St. Helena Library

DATE			

THE CALIFORNIA GOLD RUSH IN AMERICAN HISTORY

Other titles *in American History*

The Alamo
in American History
(ISBN 0-89490-770-0)

The Battle of the Little Bighorn
in American History
(ISBN 0-89490-768-9)

The California Gold Rush
in American History
(ISBN 0-89490-878-2)

The Great Depression
in American History
(ISBN 0-89490-881-2)

Japanese-American Internment
in American History
(ISBN 0-89490-767-0)

Native Americans and the Reservation
in American History
(ISBN 0-89490-769-7)

The Oregon Trail
in American History
(ISBN 0-89490-771-9)

The Transcontinental Railroad
in American History
(ISBN 0-89490-882-0)

The Underground Railroad
in American History
(ISBN 0-89490-885-5)

IN AMERICAN HISTORY

THE CALIFORNIA GOLD RUSH IN AMERICAN HISTORY

Linda Jacobs Altman

Enslow Publishers, Inc.

44 Fadem Road   PO Box 38
Box 699   Aldershot
Springfield, NJ 07081   Hants GU12 6BP
USA   UK

Library of Congress Cataloging-in-Publication Data

Altman, Linda Jacobs, 1943–
    The California gold rush in American history / Linda Jacobs Altman.
        p. cm. — (In American history)
    Includes bibliographical references (p.) and index.
    Summary: Describes adventures and disasters in the lives of people who rushed to the gold mines of California in 1848 and explains how this event sparked the state's development.
    ISBN 0-89490-878-2
    1. California—Gold discoveries—Juvenile literature. 2. California—History—1846–1850—Juvenile literature. [1. California—Gold discoveries. 2. California—History—1846–1850.] I. Title. II. Series.
F865.A46   1997
979.4'04—DC21   96-54262
                                                          CIP
                                                          AC

Illustration Credits: California Department of Parks and Recreation; Photographic Archives, pp. 73, 116; Courtesy of the California History Room, California State Library, Sacramento, California, pp. 6, 11, 16, 21, 23, 29, 34, 37, 42, 48, 50, 52, 62, 65, 80, 89, 94, 101, 105, 110, 113, 117; Library of Congress, p. 46.

Cover Illustration: Courtesy of the California History Room, California State Library, Sacramento, California; Library of Congress.

★ CONTENTS ★

The yearning for that one "big strike" motivated the forty-niner's daily work and haunted his nightly dreams.

THOSE GOLDEN HILLS

G old! In 1848, that magic word started a whole nation dreaming. Gold was discovered in California—enough for everybody, with plenty left to spare. The news spread across the country, triggering one of the most amazing migrations in history.

People came by sea in anything they could get to float from sleek clipper ships to converted whalers. They came by wagon, over the prairies and through the mountains. One enterprising fellow piled all his worldly possessions in a wheelbarrow and walked, whistling "Yankee Doodle" as he went. He whistled and walked and pushed his way to Salt Lake City, Utah, where he finally joined a wagon train rather than cross the Sierra Mountains alone.

Hundreds, even thousands, who started the trip did not live to finish it. Those who made it all the way to "Californy" found a harsh reality, which failed to match their dreams. The mining towns were rude and crude, the work was backbreaking.

People from many places and many walks of life came together in a common enterprise. All too often, they met as competitors rather than friends. Lawlessness and trickery ran rampant, and nonwhites were especially vulnerable to attack. In the mid-1800s most white Americans considered themselves superior to African Americans, Asians, Latinos, Native Americans, and anybody else whose appearance and culture differed markedly from their own. Racist language that would shock us today was part of the normal vocabulary. In this atmosphere, minorities struggled to just survive, let alone prosper.

Everything seemed fast in gold country. The population boomed. Businesses came and went. Miners made a fortune one day and lost it the next. Whole towns grew up overnight and disappeared just as quickly. People lived hard, played hard, and too often, died hard.

California made a magnificent stage for this drama. With deserts and mountains along its eastern border and an ocean to the west, it possessed a larger-than-life, mythic quality that went beyond the lure of gold. Even its name was the stuff of legend. Thinking they had found the island domain of Calafía, "beautiful, black-skinned queen of the Amazons," the Spanish conquistadors named their discovery in her honor.

The story of the hardy dreamers of 1849 is shot through with outrageous legends, epic adventures, and facts that seem a good deal stranger than fiction. Perhaps that is why it remains as fascinating today as it was when a generation of Americans set off to conquer those golden hills.

A Gentleman of Substance

When California belonged to Mexico, it was elegant, aristocratic, and unfailingly hospitable—a land of adobe ranch houses and flamenco guitars, of ladies in lace headdresses, and of gentlemen who never sullied their hands with manual labor, or worried much about anything so vulgar as money. This was the California that attracted John Sutter. He dreamed of power, prestige, and enough land to build an empire. He could not possibly guess that finding gold would one day destroy that dream.

Johann August Sutter was born on February 15, 1803, in the German village of Kandern. His parents were Swiss working folk who lived in comfortable obscurity. Jakob Sutter worked as foreman of the Kandern papermill, a position his father had held before him. The family expected Johann to follow in the old traditions, but the imaginative young man had other ideas. He hopped from place to place and job to job, looking for work that would suit him. He found a wife instead. On October 24, 1826, he married Anna Dubeld of Burgdorf; the next day she gave birth to their first son. This instant family had a significant impact on Sutter. For a time, he made an honest effort to settle down and tend to his responsibilities.

To help him along, Sutter's new mother-in-law set him up in the drygoods business. He brought tremendous energy to the project, along with a willingness to work and a buoyant faith in his own abilities. Unfortunately, he also brought an appalling lack of business savvy. He wanted to go too far, too fast, and his impatience cost him dearly.

After four years of mismanagement, the business teetered on the edge of bankruptcy and Sutter faced financial disaster. In the 1830s, debtor's prison was the fate of a man who could not pay his bills. Johann Sutter got out of the country one step ahead of the police, leaving his wife and children to fend for themselves. In the summer of 1834, he landed in New York, with the past securely behind him and a new continent ahead.

Sutter was the sort of charming rascal who could sell sand in the desert, and while he was not an out-and-out thief, he was not overly concerned about the ethics of his schemes. The newness of America appealed to him; here, he could escape his working-class origins and become the person he longed to be.

John Sutter was not interested in gold. Instead he dreamed of becoming a land baron, with vast holdings and a respected name.

He Americanized his name from "Johann" to "John" and set about building a new and distinguished identity for himself. He wove that identity from the bits and pieces of his life: a few stray facts and half-truths, generously seasoned with daydreams and fantasies. So it was that the indifferently educated son of a Swiss papermill foreman became "Captain" John A. Sutter, highborn veteran of the Royal Swiss Guards, in service to King Charles X of France.

Sutter spent freely to surround himself with an aura of wealth and privilege. He dressed well, entertained lavishly, and became so expert at playing the aristocratic adventurer that he probably believed his own charade. During his first five years in America, Sutter crossed the continent, visited Russian holdings in the Northwest and sailed to Hawaii. Along the way he ingratiated himself with several wealthy Americans, one Russian admiral, and a king—Kamehameha III of Hawaii.

A thoroughly convincing Captain John A. Sutter arrived in California with borrowed money, a contingent of Hawaiian workers he had hired and brought from the islands, and a sheaf of glowing letters describing him as a man of substance, character, and leadership ability. Sutter made his first landfall in California at Yerba Buena ("good herb"), on the northern coast. It was a scruffy, scrawny place with nothing special about it except a natural harbor.

Richard Henry Dana painted a bleak portrait of it in *Two Years Before the Mast*:

> It was in the winter of 1835–6 that the ship Alert . . . floated into the vast solitude of the Bay. . . . Our anchorage was between a small island, called Yerba Buena and a . . . cove of the same name. . . . Beyond, to the westward of the landing place, were dreary sand-hills, with little grass to be seen, and few trees, and beyond them higher hills, steep and barren, their sides gullied by the rains. Some five or six miles beyond the landing-place, to the right, was a ruinous Presidio [garrison], and some three or four miles to the left was the Mission of Dolores, as ruinous as the Presidio. . . . Vast banks of fog, invading us from the North Pacific, drove in through the entrance, and covered the whole bay; and when they disappeared, we saw a few well-wooded islands, the sand-hills on the west, the grassy and wooded slopes on the east, and the vast stretch of the bay to the southward. . . . On the whole coast of California there was not a lighthouse, a beacon, or a buoy, and the charts were made up from old and disconnected surveys by British, Russian, and Mexican voyagers.[1]

John Sutter saw the same landscape when he sailed into the harbor of Yerba Buena, but instead of desolation, he saw opportunity. Sutter was not known for his good judgment in matters of business, but this time he was absolutely right. Sutter himself would be part of events that transformed the grimy village of Yerba Buena into the world-class city of San Francisco.

Sutter moved inland, seeking fertile flatlands where he could build himself a new-world version of a feudal empire. By 1847, he had turned a dream into a Mexican land grant of some fifty thousand acres. The Spanish had established themselves in the new world by first claiming territory for Spain, then awarding huge land grants to pioneering settlers. Mexico continued the practice after it became an independent republic in 1822. Grants usually went to Mexican citizens, but John Sutter was the kind of lofty dreamer the government wanted in California. For him, they made an exception.

He did not disappoint them. He began building right away, starting with Sutter's Fort, a fortified settlement at the confluence of the Sacramento and American rivers. The fort was surrounded by walls of baked adobe, eighteen feet high and two and a half feet thick. Two lookout towers surveyed the delta valley and just in case of revolution, rebellion, or invasion, each one had a genuine dungeon at its base. Within the compound, there were barracks, workshops, a bakery, and a blanket factory.

Although Sutter's land grant came from Mexico, he was not one to stand on political formalities. When the United States acquired California in the Mexican War of 1846–1848, he hoisted the Stars and Stripes over the fort and continued building his empire as if he had barely noticed the change.

Sutter's fortunes soared under the American government; all roads to California seemed to lead through Sutter's Fort. Workshops turned out blankets, hats, shoes, saddles, and bridles, which found a ready market among the American settlers who were coming into the area. The possibilities seemed endless, at least they did until Sutter decided to build a sawmill on the south fork of the American River, at a place called Coloma.

One Winter's Day at Coloma

The location seemed perfect. The country around the mill site was green and golden, set like a jewel in the foothills of the magnificent Sierra Mountains. To the east, the hill country met the mountains. To the west, it met the fertile flatlands of the central valley. It was a place of clear, cold waters and abundant wildlife. Generations of Native Americans had thrived on its bounty and now John Sutter planned to make it part of his California empire.

In August 1847, Sutter hired thirty-seven-year-old carpenter and handyman James Marshall to build the sawmill. Marshall himself had scouted the site, about fifty miles northeast of Sutter's Fort. The work began in early September and continued through the fall and winter.

On January 24, 1848, Marshall was conducting a routine inspection of the millrace (water-flow channel)

This is Sutter's Mill as it looked in those fabulous days of the late 1840s.

when he saw traces of bright yellow metal. Intrigued, he sent one of his helpers for a tin pan. He scooped a handful of dirt from the edge of the channel and swirled it around in the pan. The lightweight sand and gravel spun to the outer edge and easily washed away.

James Marshall found himself staring at a tiny pile of what appeared to be pure gold. When he told the workers at the mill about his discovery, they shrugged it off. Gold just lying around in a millrace? Not very likely. Besides, James Marshall had a longstanding reputation for being "strange." He was a loner, for one thing, given to black moods and surly behavior. Rumor had it that he was a spiritualist who believed he could communicate with the dead.

Despite the skepticism of his fellow workers, Marshall continued panning samples of the gleaming metal, his unwavering enthusiasm drawing the others along, almost in spite of themselves. They carefully compared Marshall's mysterious substance to a gold coin—the color and weight seemed right. Next, they hammered some of the metal, knowing that iron pyrite (fool's gold) would splinter, while true gold would not. The test piece flattened to a thin sheet. Fire could not burn this substance, nor could lye dissolve it.

Soon everyone at the camp shared Marshall's mounting excitement. They went back to the channel to explore, to dream, and to dig. Marshall hurried to the fort to tell John Sutter what he had found. He rode through a driving rain, arriving at the fort wet through to the skin and in a state of near-frantic excitement. Sutter recalled the incident in his journal:

> He asked to see me alone in the "big house" where my private office and the clerk's office were located. I was utterly surprised, because the day before I had sent up everything he required, mill iron and provisions. I could not imagine what he wanted, yet I conducted him to my private rooms. . . . We entered and I shut the door behind me. Marshall asked me if the door was locked. "No," I replied, "but I shall gladly lock it." I knew that he was a very strange man, and I took the whole thing as a whim of his . . . I supposed he acted so queerly because he wanted to tell me some secret which he considered important.[2]

The two men agreed to keep Marshall's discovery secret until they could decide how to proceed. Sutter did not want to lose all his workers to gold fever. Even more to the point, he needed time to get title to the Coloma land. It was outside the boundary of his holdings—a detail that hardly mattered for a sawmill but could be critical for a gold strike.

Sutter worked out a lease with the Yalesumni tribe, who had lived on the land for generations. The agreement gave him control of a twelve-square-mile area around the mill, including all mining rights. He sent the document to the military governor, Richard Mason for formal approval. Unfortunately for Sutter,

SOURCE DOCUMENT

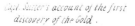

Capt. Sutter's account of the first
discovery of the Gold.

"I was sitting one afternoon," said the Captain,
"just after my siesta, engaged, by the bye, in
writing a letter to a relation of mine at Lucern,
when I was interrupted by Mr. Marshal, a gen-
tleman with whom I had frequent business
transactions - bursting hurriedly into the
room. From the unusual agitation in his
manner I imagined that something serious
had occured, and, as we involuntarily do in
this part of the world, I at once glanced to
see if my rifle was in its proper place. You
should know that the mere appearance of Mr.
Marshal at that moment in the Fort, was quite
enough to surprise me, as he had but two days
before left the place to make some alterations in a
mill for sawing pine planks, which he had just
run up for me, some miles higher up the Americ-
anos. When he had recovered himself a little, he
told me that, however great my surprise might be
at his unexpected reappearance, it would be much
greater when I heard the intelligence he had come to
bring me. 'Intelligence,' he added, 'which if properly
profited by, would put both of us in possession of
unheard-of-wealth millions and millions of dollars, in
fact.' I frankly own, when I heard this that I thought
something had touched Mr. Marshall's brain, when suddenly all my
misgivings were put at an end to by his flinging on the table a
handful of scales of pure virgin gold. I was fairly thunderstruck
and asked him to explain what all this meant, when he went on to say, that
according to my instructions, he had thrown the mill-wheel out of gear, to let the whole
body of the water in the dam find a passage through the tail race, which was previously
too narrow to allow the water to run in sufficient quantity, whereby the wheel was prevented from
efficiently performing its work. By this alteration the narrow channel was considerably enlarged, and a mass
of sand & gravel carried off by the force of the torrent. Early in the morning after this took place, Mr. Marshal
was walking along the left Bank of the stream when he perceived something which he at first took for a piece of
opal - a clair transparant stone, very common here - glittering on one of the spots laid bare by the sudden crumb-
ling away of the bank. He paid no attention to this; but while he was giving directions to the workmen, having
observed several similar glittering fragments, his curiosity was so far excited, that he stooped down & picked
one of them up. 'Do you know,' said Mr. Marshal to me, 'I positively debated within myself two or three times
whether I should take the trouble to bend my back to pick up one of the pieces and had decided on not doing
so when further on, another glittering morsel caught my eye - the largest of the pieces now before you. I
condescended to pick it up, and to my astonishment found that it was a thin scale of what appears to
be pure gold.' He then gathered some twenty or thirty pieces which on examination convinced him that
his supposition were right. His first impression was, that this gold had been lost or buried there, by
some early Indian tribe - perhaps some of those mysterious inhabitants of the west, of whom we have no
account, but who dwelt on this continent centuries ago, and built those cities and temples, the ruins
of which are scattered about these solitary wilds. On proceeding, however, to examine the neighbouring
soil, he discovered that it was more or less auriferous. This at once decided him. He mounted his
horse, and rode down to me as fast as it could carry him with the news.
At the conclusion of Mr. Marshals account, and when I had convinced myself, from the specimens he
had brought with him, that it was not exagerated, I felt as much excited as himself. I eagerly inquired
if he had shown the gold to the work people at the mill and was glad to hear that he had not spoken to a
single person about it. We agreed not to mention the circumstance to any one, and arranged to set off
early the next day for the mill. On our arrival, just before sundown, we poked the sand about in
various places, and before long succeeded in collecting between us more than an ounce of gold,
mixed up with a good deal of sand. I stayed at Mr Marshall's that night, and the next day we proceeded
some little distance up the south Fork, and found that gold existed along the whole course, not
only on the bed of the main stream, where the had subsided but in every little dried-up creek
and ravine. Indeed I think it is more plentiful in these latter places, for I myself, with nothing
more than a small knife, picked out from dry gorge, a little way up the mountain, a solid
lump of gold which weighed nearly an ounce and a half.
Notwithstanding our precautions not to be observed, as soon we came back to the mill, we noticed
by the excitement of the working people, that we had been dogged about, an to complet our desap-
pointment, some of the indians who had worked at the gold mine in the neighbourhood of la Paz
cried out in showing to us some specimens picked up by himself, — Oro! - Oro - Oro !!!—

This letter sheet illustrates the story of James Marshall and his historic discovery.

he did not get it. On March 4, Mason declared the lease invalid, on the grounds that United States law did not recognize agreements made with Native Americans by private parties.

Off to the Foothills

At Coloma, James Marshall had found the northern end of the mother lode, a single vein of gold that stretched one hundred twenty miles south to Mariposa. Geologically, it was the product of the same prehistoric upheaval that spewed great quantities of magma (molten rock) to the surface and folded layer upon layer of granite to form the mighty Sierra Mountains.

Such a discovery at Sutter's Mill could not remain secret for long. Word passed from friend to friend and acquaintance to acquaintance. A man named Sam Brannan finally blew the story wide open. Brannan was a renegade Mormon who liked wheeling and dealing better than praying and farming. The thought of gold, just lying around in riverbeds, delighted him beyond words.

On May 12, 1848, he issued a wake-up call to San Francisco by the simple strategy of walking the streets of the city, waving a bottleful of gold in the air and shouting, "Gold! Gold! Gold from the American River."

Samuel Brannan's famous announcement in the streets of San Francisco triggered mass migrations into the foothills of the Sierra Mountains.

Excited gold rushers tripped over themselves and one another to get to the foothills as quickly as possible. Merchants closed their shops, workers quit their jobs, soldiers deserted their posts. They became the "forty-eighters"—the lucky few who happened to be in the right place (northern California) at precisely the right time. On May 19, 1848, the first wave of them hit Sutter's Fort.

With simple equipment, a knack for spotting likely sites, and a dash of good California luck, a forty-eighter could amass a small fortune in placer gold. Placer refers to gold that is loose on the ground or in rivers, as opposed to vein or hardrock gold. The foothill area of the High Sierras was nature's own treasure trove of placer gold.

A typical prospecting kit included a pan, a pick, and an all-purpose shovel. When two or three miners worked together, they often used a "rocker"—a boxlike, wooden device for "washing" larger quantities of dirt. Rocking separated gold from dross (waste matter) more quickly, but it lacked precision. Careful miners panned the tailings to catch any gold the rocker left behind.

Both rocking and panning took advantage of the fact that gold is heavier than sand or gravel. Swirl the pan or rock the rocker in gently-moving water and the dross washes away, leaving the gold.

The "forty-eighters" flocked to gold country. Being the first on the scene gave them an advantage over those who would come from distant places.

Tall tales coming out of the mother lode country made prospecting sound easy: a person could just grab a handful of dirt from a riverbank, shake it around a bit in his pan, and pluck out gold nuggets as big as marbles.

The truth was more complicated. River-borne gold was not there for the taking; it had settled into holes and crevices and collected at the base of submerged boulders. A miner used his pick and shovel as much as his pan. Sometimes, a full day of backbreaking work produced only a few grains of gold.

If the work was hard and not always rewarding, the spirit of forty-eight gave it zest and meaning. A sense of adventure, of common enterprise, filled the air.

People were gold-hungry but not yet desperate enough to throw their scruples aside in the scramble for wealth. The solitary prospector with his burro, his pan, and his "poke" (canvas bag for carrying gold) became a familiar sight in the foothills. So did the mule train, transporting men and equipment into remote diggings, bringing gold back out. In spite of all this activity, the atmosphere was amazingly law-abiding and orderly.

That would change when news of the strike reached "the states," as Californians called the United States. Nobody knew what that would do to Sutter's Fort, but one thing seemed clear: It would never be the same again.

2

CALIFORNIA BOUND

Once gold fever hit the East, nothing seemed to matter but going to California. Emigrants went by land over the prairies and by sea, around Cape Horn. Some sailed down the eastern coast of the United States and Mexico. Then they traveled across the Isthmus of Panama—the thin piece of land dividing the Gulf of Mexico and the Pacific—to connect with a northbound ship.

None of the routes were easy or safe, yet for thousands of pioneers, the question was not whether to go to California but simply how best to get there.

A Good Ship and a Fair Wind

Even the most eager gold rushers thought twice about going around Cape Horn. The voyage took about six months, and led down the east coast of two continents, through the treacherous waters of the Cape, then northward to San Francisco. It was a route for the stout of heart and strong of stomach.

It attracted young, fit men with a sense of adventure, and even then, most of them traveled in organized groups rather than face the ordeal alone. These "companies" were common on all routes to gold country, but the seagoing groups tended to be more stable than their land-based counterparts. The occupants of a ship at sea could not just strike out on their own at the first sign of disagreement.

The Brothers Mining and Trading Company of New Haven, Connecticut, was typical of the associations that made the voyage in 1849. Each man put two hundred dollars into the kitty and agreed to a set of bylaws governing everything from personal conduct to division of profits. Brothers Company members pledged not to drink or gamble and not to work on the Sabbath (Sunday), except in cases of emergency. Few, if any, of these codes of conduct lasted through the voyage, let alone the rough-and-tumble gold towns of California.

The Brothers Company went to sea on May 26, 1849, aboard the *J. Walls, Jr.* Member William Ives Morgan kept a terse journal of his experiences. The events he considered noteworthy seem to support the anonymous definition of a long sea voyage as boredom interrupted by an occasional disaster. In June, he recorded the capture of a one-hundred-pound sea turtle, which was promptly slated for the ship's table.

His entry for July 4 hinted that the company had already abandoned its no drinking policy: "The Boys began to feel independent quite early. . . . [their] doings caused a regular growl aboard, and Morgan moved into the forecastle out of cabin society."[1] By August 1, the hint had become a clear statement: "The 30th being my birthday, *I got drunk!*"[2]

Morgan mentioned a sailor jumping overboard to retrieve someone's lost cap, for which he received a one-dollar reward. He recalled the general hilarity that ensued when one overly ambitious passenger tried to go whale hunting with nothing but a lifeboat and a lance.

Hazards of the Voyage

Intermixed with these events are more serious notations: the rationing of water and then of sugar, the first death on board. A poignant notation for September 18 touched upon a fear of every seafaring man: "Doctor says I have scurvy, but I don't."[3]

In 1849, doctors did not know that lack of ascorbic acid (vitamin C) caused scurvy, but they did recognize the symptoms: the bleeding gums; loosened teeth; swollen, blackened legs; chills; and delirium, all too often followed by death. They also realized that eating fresh fruits and vegetables could prevent and even cure scurvy. The problem was getting enough of the right foods in the middle of the ocean.

Food in general was a matter of great concern on shipboard: people dreamed about it, thought about it, even wrote about it. When it was good they praised it, and when it was bad they did not hesitate to protest. On one ship, the passengers and crew came close to mutiny when the captain cut their rations.

Samuel Hazelton of New Hampshire wrote home about the food aboard the brig *Randolph*:

> We shall have a good dinner [tonight]: potatoes, beef, and Duff Duff, [which] is made of flour and water with raisins mixed in and then it is put into a bag and boiled. It then makes a very palatable dish with the addition of a little sauce made from molasses and sugar. We have Duff three times a week, mush three times, rice three or four times, beans or peas twice, Mackerel or Cod Fish twice or three times. . . . There has been no sickness except sea sickness. I never felt better in my life.[4]

Good feelings generally vanished when the ship reached Cape Horn; everyone dreaded that treacherous crossing. It was the ultimate wild ride—a lurching, rolling, mast-cracking exercise in desperation that often required thirty days to complete. Ships bobbled like corks on the water while crashing waves broke over their decks.

Steamers chugged up and down the coast, making the run between Panama and San Francisco. Others operated along the Atlantic shore.

William Morgan captured the experience in his telegraphic, logbook style:

> The [ship] is taking water over both rails; everything on deck breaking loose; man hurt from beef-barrel rolling on him. Vessel heaved to, under close-reefed mainsail, and [rigging] covered with ice. Only one sail for company on this tempest of waters.[5]

The Panama Connection

Those who traveled through Panama didn't have to face the terrors of Cape Horn, but the sixty-mile wide stretch of jungle had some dangers of its own. It was a land of humid jungles, with malarial mosquitoes and cholera-infested waters. The Changres River ran two-thirds of the way across.

Most gold rushers made the river passage in dugout boats called bungos, then took a pack train the rest of the way to Panama City, on the Pacific side. Some even did that last twenty miles on foot, possessions strapped to their backs, clothes clinging to their bodies like wet rags in the steamy jungle air.

For gold rushers eager to reach the California mines, Panama was little more than an unwelcome interruption. For journalist Bayard Taylor, it was a great deal more. He was not going to California for the gold: He planned to write a book about his adventures. With this purpose in mind, he looked past

the danger and inconvenience to the wild beauty of
the land:

> There is nothing in the world comparable to these
> forests. . . . All the gorgeous growths of an eternal
> summer are so mingled in one impenetrable mass that
> the eye is bewildered. From the rank jungle of canes
> and gigantic lilies, and the thickets of strange shrubs
> that line the water, rise the trunks of the mango, the
> ceiba, the coco, the sycamore and the superb palm. . . .
> Blossoms of crimson, purple, and yellow, of a form
> and magnitude unknown in the north, are mingled
> with the leaves . . . and the brilliant butterflies circle
> through the air like blossoms blown away.[6]

In Panama City, weary travelers faced yet another
problem: Transportation on the Pacific side was a
catch-as-catch-can proposition, with tickets on
overcrowded steamships going at premium prices. As
usual, the gold rushers grumbled, struggled, and in the
end made fun of their own difficulties in doggerel
verse and comic songs like "Humbug Steamship
Companies":

> *The greatest imposition that the public ever saw,*
> *Are the California steamships that run to*
> *Panama;*
> *They're a perfect set of robbers, and accomplish*
> *their designs*
> *By a gen'ral invitation of the people to the mines.*[7]

Humbug companies notwithstanding, the route
through Panama was still the fastest way to the gold

fields. Bayard Taylor made the trip from New York City to San Francisco in fifty-one days, while William Morgan and his compatriots from the Brothers Mining and Trading Company spent six months at sea on their voyage around the Horn.

Across the Wide Missouri

The overland route required at least four months of foot-slogging danger through rough, untamed country. Timing was critical. Start before the spring grass came in, and pack animals might starve for lack of forage. Wait too long, and the company would never get through the western mountains before winter.

In early April, emigrants eager to begin their journey began assembling along the Missouri River. At Independence and St. Joseph, Missouri, and Council Bluffs, Iowa, they readied their wagons, sorted themselves into companies, and waited for the prairie grass to grow beyond the river. Ferries would take them across when the time was right, and the westward trek would begin.

People who lived along the river had seen emigrant trains assemble every spring since 1841, but nothing had prepared them for the all-out stampede of 1849. Some sixty-two hundred wagons would go over the Oregon-California Trail that season, a hefty increase over the one hundred that made the trip in 1848. That meant twenty-two thousand people, sixty thousand pack animals, and a train that would stretch for sixty miles if all the wagons formed a single line. Other overland routes, such as the Arkansas, Santa Fe, and Mexican trails, were equally congested.

Josiah and Sarah Royce were part of the great crush of humanity pressing west. Not many women made the trip in 1849. The gold rush was a man's game, or so people said. Sarah Royce seemed entirely too refined and delicate to buck the trend. This young wife and mother had education and what people used to call "breeding," meaning good manners and an unfailing sense of Victorian propriety. She also had a quiet courage that would hold her in good stead for the adventure to come:

> On the last day of April, 1849 we began our journey to California. . . . The morning . . . was not very bright; but neither was it very gloomy. . . . I would not . . . delay our departure for fear of the weather. Had I not made up my mind to encounter many storms? If we were going, let us go, and meet what we were to meet, bravely.[8]

The Royces reached Council Bluffs in late May, only to find a sprawling "city" of wagons waiting to cross the river. No cause for worry, said the ferrymen—everybody should be across in a week or so. The "week or so" stretched to three weeks by the time the Royces crossed the Missouri.

The journey across the plains was a foot-slogging endurance test for humans, animals, and equipment.

While the Royces were still struggling with ferry schedules in Council Bluffs, a larger company in St. Joseph was beginning its crossing. The Washington City and California Mining Association had so many wagons it took three days to ferry them all across the Missouri River. The leader of this well-organized group was a former West Pointer with a name that sounded like something out of a Charles Dickens novel: J. Goldsborough Bruff.

Bruff was fastidious, even fussy by some standards; the sort of leader men respected but did not especially like. He possessed an analytical mind, a discerning eye for detail, and a passion for writing things down. He kept his journals faithfully, even recording the inscription on every grave marker he saw along the trail. Unlike most of the company leaders, Bruff was in no hurry. He wanted to experience the journey as well as get to the gold. In his orderly, entirely sensible world, all things would come in time. He refused to hurry.

Life and Death on the Prairie

Grass came in thick and early on the rain-soaked plains. This proved to be a mixed blessing for the thousands of travelers headed for gold country. There was forage aplenty for the animals, but the saturated ground had an annoying way of swallowing wagon wheels. Somebody's rig was always getting stuck in the mud;

extricating it involved several strong men and a great deal of pulling, pushing, coaxing, and cursing.

People began lightening their loads so the wagons would not sink so deeply in the mud. They abandoned everything from clothes and kitchen gear to prized family heirlooms. One of the first lessons of the trail was that pioneers could not afford to be pack rats.

They also could not afford to be finicky eaters. Overland emigrants lived on a diet of biscuits and bacon, washed down with strong coffee. Most wagons also carried flour, salt, cured meats, and dried fruit. To supplement this spartan fare, people gathered wild berries and greens along the trail, caught fish in sparkling clear streams, and shot an occasional elk or buffalo for meat.

Life on the trail, particularly early on, was not all abandoned treasures and salted meat. At the end of a long day's travel, the forty-niners gathered around their campfires to share the evening meal and swap stories. Sooner or later, someone took out a banjo or maybe a fiddle, and the company began to sing. The songs of the trail were rustic, lively tunes like "Oh Susannah," unofficial anthem of the gold rush, and "Sweet Betsy from Pike":

> *Who crossed the big mountains with her lover Ike.*
> *With two yoke of cattle, a large yellow dog,*
> *A tall Shanghai rooster and one spotted hog.*[9]

Wagon encampments were lively places, especially at the beginning of the journey when everything was fresh and new.

SOURCE DOCUMENT

From a letter dated June 24, 1849:

IN THE EVENING WE ALL ASSEMBLED AND HAD AN OLD FASHIONED SING, EVERYONE SINGING THE TUNES HE KNEW AND ALL WHO COULD ASSISTING HIM. WE CARRIED THREE PARTS TO MANY TUNES OF MY ACQUAINTANCE, AND I WAS HIGHLY PLEASED AT THE FULL, SWELLING TONES OF SOME OF THE VOICES OF THE PLYMOUTH COMPANY. THE EFFECT OF THE SINGING AS IT SOUNDED ALONG THROUGH THE STILLNESS OF THE PLAINS WAS ELECTRIC ON ME, AND I SUPPOSE THE WOLVES, FOR THEY SET UP THE MOST HORRID POW-WOW ON THE PLAINS BEYOND OUR CAMP.[10]

This letter illustrates that the trip to gold country by wagon train was not all hard work and danger.

In the popular imagination, forty-niners lived in mortal terror of attack by Native Americans. Actually, there was very little "Indian trouble" on the trail in 1849. The Sioux, Cheyenne, and other prairie tribes had yet to see the interlopers as a threat to their way of life. The strangers were just passing through, after all. They did not want buffalo or land or anything else of value. All they wanted was a strange yellow metal that seemed worthless to the mighty hunters of the plains.

By far the greatest danger that year was cholera, the devastating intestinal infection that took to the trail with the forty-niners. A water-borne type of bacteria causes cholera, but no one knew that in 1849. They just knew that the disease moved swiftly, killing in a matter of days, sometimes even hours, after symptoms first appeared. The symptoms were terrifying to watch and agonizing to experience: violent vomiting, diarrhea, chills, and fever. Fluid loss caused dehydration, which made the blood thicken and body tissues begin to wither. Victims often died convulsing and delirious, faces ashen, lips a sickly blue.

The Royce company faced cholera early in their journey. One of the party died within hours of his first symptoms, leaving everyone shaken and wary. That night the wind moaned across the prairie, and a steady rain pounded the earth. The white sheet covering the body flapped in the wind.

Nearby, a group of Native Americans held a death watch of their own. Sarah watched their shadows in the flickering light of a ceremonial fire, heard their voices "chanting, hour after hour, a wild melancholy chant, varied by occasional high, shrill notes as of distressful appeal. The minor key ran through it all. I knew it was a death dirge."[11]

Despite cholera, despite everything, the great migration continued westward. It was a slow but relentless march across the grasslands to Fort Laramie in the southwest corner of present-day Wyoming. Here the country became more rugged as the trail snaked its way through the Black Hills to the eastern face of the Rocky Mountains. The immigrants went through South Pass—a broad, grassy slope rising to the Great Divide, which separates the Atlantic and Pacific watersheds.

The Place of Many Trails

Shortly below South Pass, what had been more or less a single trail splintered into several alternatives. At Fort Bridger, Wyoming, the Mormon and California-Oregon trails separated: one turning northwest to Fort Hall, Idaho, while the other continued on a southwesterly course into Salt Lake City. In addition to these basic routes, a number of shortcuts enticed tired emigrants eager to save time, mileage, or both. Sublette's Cutoff swung straight west about twenty-five miles above Fort Bridger and then rejoined the main trail. A few enterprising companies decided to try Hudspeth's Cutoff, a new trail that bypassed Fort Hall, Idaho. It was supposed to be a shortcut.

J. Goldsborough Bruff did not believe it. Hudspeth's Cutoff went through rough country; it might be a shortcut "as the crow flies," but covered wagons were noticeably lacking in wings. The ever-confident Bruff arranged for someone to measure Hudspeth's Cutoff, while he did the same to the regular route. Those who slogged their way through

rough country on an impossibly winding road were dismayed to learn that Bruff was right: Hudspeth's Cutoff measured 132.5 miles; the regular trail, 134 miles.

The members of Bruff's company did not seem impressed by their leader's shrewdness, nor grateful that he had saved them from a punishing trail. Bruff's strict ideas about company discipline, combined with his everlasting certainty, had alienated the men. They followed him as a matter of policy and enlightened self-interest, not from any loyalty or sense of affection. Bruff's moral victory at Hudspeth's Cutoff did not translate into a faster travel time. He continued the same slow, deliberate pace and the Washington City Company continued to fall behind.

Many of the trailing companies elected to go south to Salt Lake City, where they could make repairs, tend to their sick, and prepare for the grueling journey ahead. Many of these companies broke up in Salt Lake City, as some of their members decided to spend the winter in the Mormon city rather than risk freezing to death in the Sierra snows. Others decided to head for Los Angeles and spend the winter there.

Josiah and Sarah Royce made another, far more daring, choice: They headed into the heart of the Great Salt Desert, which offered their only chance of reaching the Sierras ahead of the winter snow. That was pure foolishness, said the Mormons. If they did

Well-equipped pack trains became a familiar sight in gold country. Similar trains were a favorite means of transportation across the Isthmus of Panama.

not perish from thirst in the desert, they would end up snowbound in the Sierras. Either way, they would die.

The Royces would not be dissuaded by the warnings, however well meant they might be. They left Salt Lake City on August 30, to make one last, all-or-nothing run at the gold fields.

The Promised Land

Three weeks after the Royces embarked on their fool's errand through the Salt Desert, J. Goldsborough Bruff made his first bad decision. He had heard of a shortcut that would be a safer, quicker path through the Sierras into California. With winter coming on and his company running low on supplies, the man who saw through the hoopla about Hudspeth's Cutoff could not resist Lassen's Route. Confidently, he led his people down the new trail, only to find that it ended just below the Oregon border, nowhere near the gold fields.

It was not one of Bruff's finer moments. Undoubtedly, some of the longsuffering Washington City boys could not help being pleased that the great J. Goldsborough Bruff had finally made a mistake.

The Royces fared better on their southern route, surviving the punishing journey on a combination of luck, hard work, and dogged determination. Alone on the Carson Trail, they were rescued by a relief expedition on October 12, 1849. On October 19, the Royces crested the last ridge of the Sierras. Sarah recorded the sight in her journal:

> The morning was bright and sunny. "Hope sprang exultant" for that day, that blessed 19th of October. . . . I had purposely hastened . . . to start ahead of the rest; and not far from noon, I was rewarded by coming out . . . on a rocky height whence I looked down . . . to where a soft haze sent up a warm, rosy glow that seemed to me a smile of welcome. . . . I knew I was looking across the Sacramento Valley.[12]

Thousands of others would look down on that sunlit valley and believe they had reached the promised land. Then they would head for the hills, to seek the big strike that would make the hazards and discomforts of their various journeys all worthwhile.

GREED AND DREAMS

In places like San Francisco, Sacramento, and a hundred little boomtowns scattered throughout the hills, the gold rushers shaped a way of life like none other in the world. Away from the rule of law and custom, they had to make up a society as they went along. Sometimes they succeeded and sometimes they failed. Sometimes they teetered on the edge of anarchy. The world they created might not have been conventional or even entirely "respectable," but it never ceased to be colorful.

An Odd Place, Unlike Any Other

One description of San Francisco as a strange place, unlike any other in creation, was right on the mark. San Francisco was the closest thing to an instant city that the world had ever seen. In 1848, it was a quiet port town with one thousand inhabitants. By the end of 1850, it had become a decidedly unquiet city with thirty thousand people and growing pains to match.

California during the gold rush had its own set of rules,
which did not always provide for much law and order.
Sometimes, however, gold-seekers were able to cooperate.
Here, a prospector shows newcomers how to pan for gold.

This little Spanish town that was trying to become a big American city fascinated Bayard Taylor. When he arrived in 1849 he saw:

> Hundreds of tents and houses . . . scattered all over the heights, and along the shore for more than a mile. A furious wind was blowing down through a gap in the hills, filling the streets with clouds of dust. On every side stood buildings of all kinds, begun or half-finished, and the greater part of them mere canvas sheds, open in front, and covered with all kinds of signs, in all languages. . . . The streets were full of people, hurrying to and fro, and of as diverse and bizarre a character as the houses: Yankees of every possible variety, native Californians in serapes and sombreros, Chileans, Sonorians, Chinese with long tails, Malays armed with their everlasting creeses [daggers or short swords], and others in whose . . . bearded [faces] it was impossible to recognize any special nationality.[1]

San Francisco would never lose this international flavor; over the years its merry mix of cultures would give it a reputation as a world-class city. In 1849, when city streets were quagmires of mud and public services nonexistent, that reputation seemed a long way off. William Ives Morgan sensed that San Francisco was ill-equipped to deal with the crush of humanity that descended on it in the early years of the gold rush. His journal entry for January 1, 1850, hints at the pandemonium of those early gold rush days:

> Came to anchor in harbor . . . this afternoon. Shore green and beautiful. San Francisco not so extensive as

A grizzled prospector became an enduring symbol of gold country life.

I expected; is about half tents. Mud two to four feet deep. Many murders reported. Fully 400 vessels here, and every day swells the list.[2]

The cost of goods and services stunned new arrivals. A week's worth of boardinghouse meals that would cost two dollars in the states was twenty dollars in San Francisco. The rent on a small room could run as high as fifty dollars a month. There was a recklessness in the air; a sense of intoxication with life that made everything seem fast and exciting. Would-be prospectors who had not even seen the gold country behaved like they already had a fortune.

Gold Fever

"Gold fever" was really just good old-fashioned greed, decked out in a red shirt and bandanna and topped with a floppy miner's hat. In Maine or Missouri, greed was one of the seven deadly sins. In California, it was practically respectable. One popular and often-repeated gold rush yarn reveals the gleeful way miners threw themselves into the spirit of the times.

The story begins with a group of miners gathered at the gravesite of a departed comrade. When the body was lowered into the grave:

The minister commenced [to pray], while the crowd reverently fell upon their knees. For a while, all went well; but the prayer was unnecessarily long and at last some of the congregation began, in an abstracted way,

Rough-hewn cabins like this one were common in the early towns that developed with the start of the gold rush.

to finger the loose earth that had been thrown up from the grave. It proved to be thick with gold, and an excitement was immediately apparent in the kneeling crowd. Upon this the preacher stopped and . . . took a view of the ground for himself and, as he did so, shouted "Gold! Gold!—and the richest kind of diggings! The congregation is dismissed!" The dead miner was taken from his . . . grave to be buried elsewhere, while the funeral party, with the minister at their head, lost no time in prospecting and staking out new diggings![3]

Them Thar Hills!

The first gold towns were little more than clusters of canvas tents and ramshackled wood cabins, with colorful names like Whiskey Slide, Suckertown, Helltown, and Poverty Flat. Each had its gambling hall and saloon; its prostitutes, public drunks, and habitual gamblers. A few of these early towns would outlive their disreputable beginnings to become settled communities like Marysville, Placerville, and Coloma, which still exist today.

Sarah and Josiah Royce first reached the Pleasant Valley Gold Mines, a settlement that had once been important enough to appear in their guidebook to the gold country. It was already dying when they arrived on October 24, 1849. Only a scattering of tents were left, inhabited by a few men with their panning equipment. The diggings were almost worked out,

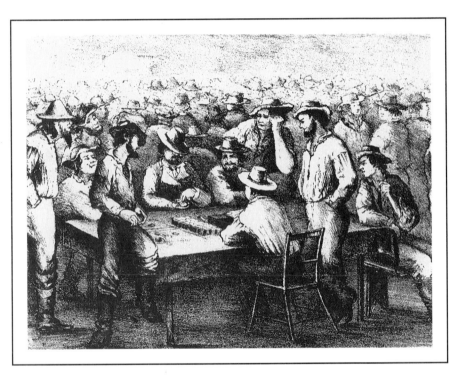

Gambling was the favored recreation in gold country. One Saturday night at the tables cost many a prospector his earnings for the entire week.

they said, but rumor had it that the diggings were rich toward Weaver Creek.

The Royces rested at the Pleasant Valley mine for a few days, then decided to try their luck in Weaverville. By gold rush standards, it had turned into a real town, complete with stores, dwellings, and, of course, the ever-present gambling hall and saloon. It was a village made of canvas rather than brick or wood. The Royces pitched their tent on a likely looking piece of property and set up housekeeping.

By the time the forty-niners made it to the gold country, only a few of the eastern "mining companies" remained intact. Miners who had been in the hills for a while liked to operate in small teams: three or four "pards" (partners) splitting the work and the wages.

A typical day began at sunup, with bitter coffee and hard biscuits for breakfast. Then it was on to the claim, where the men took turns digging with pick and shovel, washing the dirt in the rocker, and carefully bagging the gold. For ten to twelve hours of this backbreaking work, the pards would be lucky to earn fifteen dollars apiece. After twilight, they would drag themselves home for a supper of pickled pork and coffee. The lucky ones had beans or potatoes to go along with the meat.

When darkness fell, there was nothing left for the miners to do but go to sleep or head for the gambling

---

SOURCE DOCUMENT

THE MINER'S DREAM

Bright gleaming Gold! How I sought it!
I picked and dug like a slave.

Hunger and Hardship—I got it.
And now I am nearing the grave.

Yet the glittering thing still is haunting
Alluring. elusive. so near.

The lure of the gold lust is taunting.
The pan worth a million is here! [4]

After dark, miners could participate in the disreputable activities of the mining towns, or they could go to sleep and dream about the possibility of striking it rich.

---

tent where rotgut whiskey, poker, and noise helped to pass the time. Many a lonely miner dropped a day's earnings in a few short hours of "raisin' Cain" and pretending to enjoy himself.

Hunkerin' Down for Winter

A few days after the Royce family arrived safely in Weaverville, a snowstorm blocked off the passes in the high Sierras. The much-dreaded winter had finally arrived, and it promised to be a stormy one. Those who had made it through the mountains knew that anyone stranded in those snow-covered passes would face a life-or-death struggle.

J. Goldsborough Bruff was one of those unfortunates who got trapped in the mountains, but as usual, he did it in his own inimitable style. Having erred in choosing Lassen's Route, he felt duty-bound to repair as much of the damage as possible. It would not be easy. The company was a shadow of its former self—down to six wagons with only one mule team for each. The chilly air and slate-gray sky hinted that the season's first snowfall could begin any day.

At the rate they were moving, Bruff knew he could not get everyone to safety before the food ran out or the snows set in. All his precise planning, his rigorous discipline, came down to one last gamble: the main body of the company would go ahead, taking four wagons and the strongest mules. Bruff would stay behind, guarding the other wagons until someone could return with fresh animals and supplies. He even lent them his horse on the solemn promise that it would be promptly returned.

Six members of the Washington City Company came back for Bruff, but they did not seem to care one way or another about him. There were no warm greetings, no signs of concern for the man who had led them through six months of hard travel and close escapes. To add insult to injury, they had not returned his horse.

It was still in the valley, they told him. Bruff exploded in self-righteous fury, accusing his former comrades of stealing his horse and taking advantage of his good nature. He refused to return with them or even to accept the provisions they brought.

That was October 28; on October 31, it began to snow.

Sutter's Last Stand

While J. Goldsborough Bruff was destroying his last chance to escape the mountains before winter, an equally unyielding John Sutter was clinging to a faded dream. Gullibility, mismanagement, and overconfidence had cost him a good portion of his assets. The crush of humanity passing through his lands slaughtered his cattle and generally treated his holdings as if they were public property. He piled up debts, then sold off assets to pay them.

Sutter still owned the fort and most of the acreage around it, a farm on the Feather River, and a tract of land south of the Sacramento River docks. On this last site, he wanted to build the city of Sutterville; a planned community that would become the crown jewel of the entire central valley.

It was Sutter's twenty-two-year-old son August who inadvertently destroyed that dream. August had come to California in the autumn of 1848, to join the father he scarcely remembered. Seeing the terrible state of the elder Sutter's financial affairs, he set to work trying to untangle them. He was doing a fair job of it until the opportunistic Sam Brannan stepped into the picture.

While Sutter was away from home, Brannan convinced August to abandon plans for a town at the "Sutterville" site and block out a new city nearer to the fort. They would call it "Sacramento City," Brannan said, and sale of lots would pay off the family debt. In this, he was correct; lots sold so quickly that August settled the major debts in a matter of weeks. The young man was enormously pleased with himself— until his father got home.

Sutter was furious with August for abandoning his precious project. Having caused the breach, whether by accident or design, Sam Brannan could not resist jumping into it. Without August standing watchdog over the family holdings, Brannan tricked a drunken John Sutter out of his remaining holdings in Sacramento City.

The heartbroken old pioneer retreated to his farm on the Feather River. There he hid away, drinking himself into a state of numbness, as his life spun out of control. He came out of this self-imposed exile for the Constitutional Convention that began in September 1849. Prominent Californians came from all over the territory to hammer out a constitution for the proposed state. By this time, Sutter was showing the effects of growing alcoholism, but he still managed to conduct himslef with reasonable dignity. He even agreed to run for governor of the soon-to-be state of California.

Bayard Taylor met Sutter briefly during the convention. His description was a good deal kinder than many others of that period:

> Captain Sutter's appearance and manners quite agreed with my preconceived ideas of him. He is still the hale, blue-eyed, jovial German—short and stout of stature, with broad forehead, head bald to the crown, and altogether a ruddy, good-humored expression of countenance. He is a man of good intellect, excellent common sense, and amiable qualities of heart. A little more activity and enterprise might have made him the first man in California in point of wealth and influence.[5]

In this last opinion, Taylor was probably off the mark. Sutter had "activity and enterprise" to spare; it was judgment that he lacked. He had a flair for starting new endeavors. When there were ideas to express, plans to develop, and people to convince, John Sutter was in his element. He had neither the training nor the patience for the long haul.

In a three-man race for governor, Sutter came in dead last. Such a resounding defeat left little doubt that he was no longer a power in California. At the age of forty-seven, he had become a relic of bygone days, whose chief claim to fame was that he once decided to build a mill at Coloma on the American River.

Matters of Survival

Disaster followed upon disaster in the winter of 1849–50; no place in gold country seemed immune. There was fire in San Francisco and flood in Sacramento. In the isolated mining towns of the hills, dozens of people came down with scurvy because they could not get the proper foods to prevent it. Further north, those who had followed the ill-starred Lassen Route battled for survival in the mountain snow. For many a desperate gold rusher, Christmas in 1849 was anything but a season of joy.

On Christmas Eve day, wind-driven flames wiped out most of San Francisco. The city's canvas tents and wooden buildings went up like oil-soaked kindling in a blaze so fierce the flames could be seen for miles. Bayard Taylor was aboard a freighter on the first leg of his journey home when he turned for a last look at San Francisco:

> As I [looked] shoreward, a little spark appeared through the fog. Suddenly it shot up into a spiry flame and at the same instant I heard the sound of gongs, bells, and trumpets and the shouting of human voices. The calamity, predicted and dreaded so long in advance that men ceased to think of it, had come at

last—San Francisco was on fire! The blaze increased with fearful rapidity. In fifteen minutes it had risen into a broad, flickering column. . . . The roar and tumult swelled, and above the clang of gongs and the cries of the populace I could hear the crackling of blazing timbers, and the smothered sound of falling roofs.[6]

Some twenty miles down the coast, Taylor's ship began to leak. While crewmen patched and bailed, the captain turned back to San Francisco for emergency repairs. It took three days of sailing against the wind to get there.

Taylor immediately went to see what had happened in the city. He expected to see piles of rubble and the blackened carcasses of innumerable buildings. Instead he saw something so astounding, he could only shake his head in admiration:

Three days only had elapsed since the fire, yet in that time all the rubbish had been cleared away, and the frames of several houses were half raised. All over the burnt space sounded one incessant tumult of hammers, axes, and saws.[7]

The infant city might be crude, but no one could say its people lacked courage.

Miraculously, there were no deaths in the San Francisco fire, but the devastating flood in Sacramento claimed untold hundreds of victims. Sacramento sits in a vast flood plain between two rivers. Today a system of levees, reservoirs, and drainage channels protects the city, but in 1850 there was nothing.

The first rains came in December, cold and insistent; pounding the ground, swelling the rivers. This was followed by a false spring, which began melting the Sierra snowpack, releasing even more water into the valley below. Then, in January, the big storm hit.

Sarah and Josiah Royce found themselves in the middle of this disaster, having moved to Sacramento after two months of roughing it in Weaverville. On the evening of January 9, it began. The Royces took refuge on the second floor of a neighbor's newly built house.

By morning, all of Sacramento was underwater. The Royces climbed out of an upstairs window into a boat and made their way downriver to San Francisco. There they joined hundreds of other refugees seeking shelter in an already overcrowded city. The fact that they found a place to stay is a tribute to the recuperative powers of San Francisco; the Royces arrived just three weeks after the great fire of 1849.

In the snowbound Sierra Mountains, a smaller, almost unnoticed life-or-death drama ran its course. J. Goldsborough Bruff found himself in terrible straits after he sent his former companions packing. His food was almost gone, his body racked with pain from rheumatism, his camp nearly buried in snow. People still passed, but they were stragglers without food or supplies to share with anyone. Most traveled on foot, stumbling through the snow in a last, desperate effort to reach the settlements before frostbite or scurvy turned them into nameless victims of a brutal migration.

With what strength he had left, Bruff managed to act like himself, stage-managing life for any passersby who seemed to need it. He lectured an ex-army officer for burdening his two little girls with heavy packs while he himself carried only a rifle. Later, he scolded a man named Lambkin for neglecting his four-year-old

The hardy souls who wintered in the mountains were constantly digging their way out of enormous snowdrifts.

son. Bruff found the child lying in a filthy shelter, hungry and half-frozen.

Before he quite knew what was happening, he had promised to care for the little boy while his father went in search of provisions. Bruff never saw Lambkin again.

The child, William, was hollow-eyed and strangely passive, as if he had long ago given up expecting anything from life. He spoke little, and when he cried it was high and thin, a ghostly wail. In spite of Bruff's best efforts to care for him, he died on New Year's Day, 1850. Bruff gave him a decent burial and an unforgettable grave marker:

> WILLIAM, Infant son of LAMBKIN,
> An unnatural father.
> Died January 1, 1850 [8]

J. Goldsborough Bruff survived his terrible winter. He even made it to mining country, but he never struck gold. After only five months, he grew tired of the whole adventure. In the spring of 1851, he returned to Washington, D.C., where he lived a full and contented life, dying at the ripe old age of eighty-five. No one knows what happened to Lambkin.

THIS ROUGH JUSTICE

Gold rush California attracted more than its share of people possessing what is commonly called a "past"—misfits and outcasts seeking a place where yesterday didn't matter, tomorrow didn't exist, and it was easy to get lost in the crowd. In the early days, these people were often basically harmless ne'er-do-wells escaping from unpaid debts or abandoned wives. As the gold rush wore on, they were more likely to be hardened criminals, drawn by the absence of formal law and social structure as well as the promise of gold. Violence, which had been of the rowdy, bar-brawling sort, turned vicious and deliberate. Even respectable citizens grew accustomed to the sight of death.

As usual, Californians found a way to laugh about the problem, thanks to the songwriter who penned a little ditty called "What Was Your Name in the States?":

> Oh, what was your name in the States?
> Was it Thompson or Johnson or Bates?
> Did you murder your wife
> And flee for your life?
> Oh, what was your name in the States?[1]

Free-for-all claim disputes erupted frequently in the later days of the gold rush, when the hills were more crowded and the miners more desperate.

That Memorable Autumn

In early autumn of 1850, excited San Franciscans awaited news on California's petition for statehood. Sarah Royce recorded the historic moment when the steamship *Carolina* made a grand entrance into San Francisco harbor, flags flying,

> and above them, straightened out by the generous wind which seemed to blow a long breath on purpose, floated the longest streamer of all, displaying the words "California Admitted"! The roar of cannon rolled over the waters, and met answering roars from fort and ships. Everybody was laughing.[2]

The news of statehood spread through gold country. It came by word of mouth to remote mining towns and by steamer to Sacramento. The ship brought more than news to the central valley; it brought a passenger who had been infected with cholera. The man died on October 20, and the next day, several new cases were reported in various sections of the city. By October 25, the outbreak raged through Sacramento, as fast as a San Francisco fire. The healthy pushed themselves to the point of exhaustion to care for the sick and bury the dead. Before the epidemic ran its course, it had killed nine hundred people.

For many gold rushers, the cholera outbreak was the last straw. They had endured fire, flood, hunger, and epidemic disease in the desperate hope of finding gold; enough was enough. As autumn gave way to winter, one discouraged miner after another gave up the hunt and sought employment or started a business of his own. Some just wanted to go home. While they were packing to leave, several thousand easterners were preparing to set out for California with the coming of the prairie grass in the spring.

In the early 1850s, mining towns began to acquire some small comforts. A man could soak his weary body at a bathhouse, get a decent meal at a restaurant, or take in a play when a traveling theater company came to town. He could even go dancing at one of the wildly popular "fandango houses" (dance halls, named after a sensuous Mexican dance), where hired hostesses were on hand to act as partners. What he could not do was escape the seamier side of gold country life or the threat of violence that grew with each passing day and every toppled dream.

The Streets of San Francisco

As the principal ocean port of gold country, San Francisco had more than its share of brawling, swindling, gunfighting, and outright thievery. This random lawlessness took an ominous turn into professional crime when the "Sydney Ducks" appeared on the scene. They were ex-convicts from the infamous Botany Bay prison colony in Australia, career criminals who worked in gangs and had no aversion to violence.

The gold rush drew hundreds of them to San Francisco from the Australian ports of Sydney, Adelaide, and Hobart. They soon decided that crime was easier and a good deal more profitable than panning for gold.

The Sydney Ducks congregated along the waterfront at the foot of Telegraph Hill, in a district called "Sydneytown." It was a place of booze halls, gambling dens, and cheap rooming houses, avoided by respectable citizens and anyone else who valued his life. By night, the flickering light of a thousand oil lamps gave the streets a sickly glow, and enormous rats scurried through the shadows.

Crime, like the rats, ran out of control, spreading from Sydneytown to the rest of the city. The authorities seemed unwilling or unable to do anything about it, leaving honest citizens to defend themselves as best as they could. Often, that meant staying off the streets past a certain hour, never carrying sizeable amounts of cash, and knowing how to handle yourself in a fight. Like many bad situations, this one was allowed to carry on, largely because nobody knew exactly what to do about it.

Then on the evening of February 19, 1851, a particularly daring and brutal robbery galvanized the citizenry into action. It happened on busy Montgomery Street, where the shops stayed open after dark. Among the crowd of honest shoppers, a gang of Sydney Ducks went looking for likely targets.

E. M. "Old Jack" Morgan and a slick ex-forger named James Stuart entered Charles Jansen's drygoods store with a homemade Australian weapon called a "slung-shot." It was a chunk of lead tied in a folded piece of cloth. The assailant used the cloth as a sling, snapping the lead weight at the victim's head with a practiced flip of the wrist.

In the drygoods store that night, the slung-shot felled the proprietor without a sound. The robbers grabbed the cash box and escaped into the street. The Ducks made $1,586 for their night's work. The shopkeeper ended up in the hospital with a concussion, his face bruised and swollen from the blow.

Justice by Another Name

By morning, the San Francisco business community was up in arms. When honest folk were not safe on a busy street in the middle of town, it was time to take drastic action.

An anonymous handbill began to appear on the streets:

CITIZENS OF SAN FRANCISCO

Are we to be robbed and assassinated in our domiciles, and the law to let our aggressors [walk] the streets merely because they have furnished a straw bail? If so, let "each man be his own executioner." "Fie upon your laws"; they have no force.

All those who would rid our city of its robbers and murderers will assemble on Sunday [the next day] at two o'clock, on the Plaza.[3]

San Francisco stood close to mob rule, as otherwise peaceable citizens called for a lynching. Through an intricate series of moves and countermoves, William Windred and a man identified as James Stuart, were charged with the crime and dragged before a "people's court."

Windred said he was not anywhere near Jansen's store on the night in question. The man identified as Stuart claimed to be a victim of mistaken identity; his name was not James Stuart, he said, but Thomas Berdue. From his hospital room, a groggy Charles Jansen, vision blurred from the concussion, identified them as his assailants. The fact that "Stuart" insisted he was Berdue mattered little to the zealous citizens, who felt sure they had the right man.

Everyone expected a guilty verdict followed immediately by a hanging. They did not get it. In a stunning reversal of expectation, the vigilante court acquitted the defendants, on the grounds that Jansen had not seen his assailants well enough to make a positive identification.

The San Francisco newspapers took this as a sign that a "people's court," acting outside the established legal system, could indeed dispense fair and impartial rulings. That opinion probably revealed more about the depth of public fear of crime than it did about the qualifications of the vigilance committtee. The committee members were neither elected officials nor professional law enforcement officers. There was not a single lawyer among them.

Nonetheless, the *Pacific News* called the trial:

One of the most impressive demonstrations of the power and majesty of the people we ever looked upon, and one which will be long remembered among the important events of San Francisco. This was not the assembling of a mob—it was not a whirlwind of ungovernable popular fury; but it was composed of the whole body of our citizens, of every class, and of every calling.[4]

Three weeks later, a legally constituted jury found the defendants guilty, based upon the same identification by Jansen. Windred was sentenced to ten years in prison. Things went harder with the man thought to be Stuart.

While he was on trial in San Francisco, Marysville police had a warrant for the arrest of "James Stuart" on a charge of murder. After being sentenced to fourteen years in prison for the Jansen robbery, the hapless Thomas Berdue was taken to Marysville to stand trial for murder.

San Franciscans went back to their normal lives, secure in the knowledge that justice had been done. Then, at 11:00 P.M. on May 3, the city caught fire. By morning, the entire business district and most of Sydneytown lay in ruins. San Franciscans were becoming painfully accustomed to watching their city burn. This was the fourth major blaze since the one that laid waste to the city in December of 1849.

This time, many people suspected arson. For one thing, the timing was suspicious; exactly one year earlier, on May 4, 1850, fire had struck the city. To call that anniversary a coincidence seemed to stretch the bounds of common sense. Another circumstance that pointed toward arson was the widespread looting that attended this particular fire. It was almost as if the flames had been a diversion so thieves could ransack the city.

A frightened populace demanded action. If official agencies could not handle San Francisco's crime problem, then it was time for the citizens themselves to take action. A people's court had distinguished itself in the Jansen case; why not form a permanent committee to keep law and order in the city? On June 9, 1851, after long deliberation and debate, 103 of the city's leading citizens created the Committee of Vigilance to dispense swift justice and drive criminals from the city by whatever means necessary. One of the principal

Portable cages like this one were often the only jail cells available in gold country.

organizers was Sam Brannan, who had made a fortune in real estate since taking over John Sutter's Sacramento properties. The committee was disbanded in September 1851.

The Law of the Hills

Most mining towns had no formal laws, no police, and no jails. An informal "miner's code" served as a guide to the rights and responsibilities of the individual. Beyond that, it was vigilante justice, with barbaric punishments even for relatively minor crimes.

A popular, tongue-in-cheek tract called "The Miners' Ten Commandments," included such gems as "Thou shalt have no other claim than one," and "Thou shalt not grow discouraged, nor think of going home before thou hast made thy 'pile.'" It also contained a chilling warning about the punishment awaiting anyone who dared to break the code:

> Thou shalt not . . . steal from thy cabin-mate his gold dust, to add to thine, for he will . . . discover what thou hast done, and will straightaway call his fellow miners together, and if the law hinder them not they will hang thee, or give thee fifty lashes, or shave thy head and brand thee . . . upon thy cheek, to be known and read of all men . . .

These punishments were not products of the writer's imagination; they were real. People caught

The "Miners' Ten Commandments" letter sheets were part joke, part serious statement. Practically every mining cabin had a copy tacked to the wall.

stealing really were flogged or branded; those accused of murder or armed robbery could be declared guilty and hanged without benefit of judge, jury, or defense attorney.

Not only did this lynch-mob mentality kill the innocent, it often let the guilty go free. Its standards of justice were decidedly strange. After a gunfight, the fact that the loser was a corpse did not necessarily mean that the winner was a murderer. If the fight had been fair by frontier standards and the combatants reasonably well matched, then the townsfolk often refused to get involved.

The town of Sonora, California, became legendary as a place where violence went unpunished and even unnoticed. Storekeeper William Perkins kept an ongoing tally of Sonora's body count in the summer of 1850: four in the third week of June, six in the second week of July; a knifing here, a shooting there, a dead body dumped on someone's doorstep.

The modern town of Placerville also had a colorful history. It began as a mining camp called Dry Diggings and later became known as Hangtown. The name originated in the grisly story of three thieves. In a model of gold rush justice, they were caught, judged guilty by an informal citizen's committee, and promptly hanged.

Scoundrels, Scalawags, and Natural-Born Fools

In the atmosphere of greed and violence that surrounded the quest for gold, bands of desperados roamed the hills, taking what they wanted from people too weak to resist. They obeyed no law, served no social ideal, bowed to no authority but their own.

Richard Barter was an industrious, reasonably honest young miner, who turned to crime after being falsely accused of two thefts. Although he was acquitted both times, the charges had tarnished his good name. People figured he must have done something wrong; why else would a man be twice arrested for theft? The stigma clung to Barter like the odor of cheap whiskey or bad cigars.

Apparently, the young man decided that if he had the name, he might as well live up to it. As Rattlesnake Dick, Pirate of the Placers, he ranged through the hills, breaking into houses and stores, raiding small mining camps, and waylaying travelers who looked as if they might have something worth stealing.

Rattlesnake Dick was strictly small time. On his one attempt at big-league outlawry, Dick got his hands on a gold shipment only to be arrested for stealing the mules he needed to transport it. Half the gold was recovered; the other half was buried by one of Dick's accomplices, who died before he could reveal the location. Rattlesnake Dick never saw the gold. Having failed miserably at big-time robbery, the unlucky bandit went back to petty thievery, roaming free until the day sheriff's deputies spotted him near the town of Auburn.

Both Dick and another man fled in a hail of bullets, seeming to get away clean. The next day, passing travelers found the Pirate of the Placers lying dead in the road. There were two bullets in his body and a third through his brain. The deputies might have fired the first two, but they had not fired the third. That last bullet made the inept Pirate of the Placers into a genuine gold rush legend. Who fired it and why? Dick was already dying from his other wounds, so the third bullet was not necessary. Perhaps it was a mercy shot from that unknown companion; perhaps not. There was simply no way to know.

While Rattlesnake Dick became a footnote to history because of gold he never saw and a death nobody could explain, a far more dangerous bandit roamed the California hills. To some, Joaquin Murieta was nothing but a vicious killer; to others, he was Robin Hood reborn, come to avenge the wrongs of the Mexican people.

Murieta was born in Sonora, Mexico, the son of respectable parents who gave him a good education. The young man was tall and handsome, with effortless charm and a high-spirited zest for adventure. In 1848, he married his sweetheart, whose name is variously reported as Carmela or Rosita or Antonia. Some months later, he received a letter from his older brother Carlos in California: come quickly, it said, there's gold to be had in the mountains. With his young wife at his side, Murieta began the journey that would one day change his fate. In California, he found a frontier society where Mexicans were despised as an inferior people, and justice was an uncertain thing.

For Joaquin Murieta, it was a nonexistent thing. His brother was lynched by a mob that hated Mexicans, his wife raped and murdered, and Murieta himself publicly flogged and humiliated when a horse he had borrowed turned out to be stolen. These images of horror haunted his mind and turned a peaceable young man into a bloodthirsty desperado.

From the beginning of Murieta's criminal career to its bloody end, fact and legend became hopelessly entangled. Every robbery, ambush, or unsolved murder was attributed to Joaquin Murieta and his gang. Death only made his legend grow.

On July 30, 1853, the *San Francisco Herald* reported that a company of state rangers under the command of Captain Harry Love had hunted down and killed Joaquin Murieta along with his most feared accomplice; a demonic killer known only as "Three-Fingered Jack."

Joaquin Murieta was a vicious outlaw to some, a folk hero to others. His story is one of the enduring legends of gold rush California.

To prove that the legendary bandits had indeed met their end, Captain Love cut off the head of Murieta and the hand of Three-Fingered Jack. Both were preserved in alcohol and widely exhibited around the state—grisly trophies of a time and a place where the rules of civilized society did not apply.

5

UNEQUAL OPPORTUNITY

Americans in the 1850s believed in manifest destiny, the notion that the United States had the duty and the right to expand its territory and influence in North America. It was a handy doctrine because it justified so many things: forcing Native Americans off their land, fighting a territorial war with Mexico, excluding "foreigners" from full participation in the social, economic, and political life of the nation.

The gold discovery that had caused such rejoicing in the states triggered a very different reaction among Native Americans and Californios (Spanish-speaking Mexicans who had lived in California since it belonged to Mexico). They watched with sadness as wave upon wave of gold-hungry immigrants transformed the land they loved into something they no longer recognized.

The new arrivals never questioned their right to claim the land, the gold, and whatever else they wanted. Manifest destiny justified everything and was itself justified by the notion that whites were inherently superior to others and therefore entitled to rule over them. This view shaped the way white Americans treated people of other racial and cultural backgrounds. Native peoples, African Americans, Latinos, and Chinese faced an uphill struggle just to survive in gold rush California, let alone to succeed and prosper.

The Native Americans

Europeans who transplanted their civilization to the new world saw no value in the tribal cultures they encountered there. They called these cultures inferior and swept them away, secure in the belief that they were "civilizing" a savage land. The gold rush accelerated this cultural destruction by bringing thousands of wagons across the Great Plains. This contempt for native lifestyles was so pervasive that even the humane, deeply religious Sarah Royce could speak quite unself-consciously about dealing with the "begging and pilfering Indians" who roamed the encampment at Council Bluffs: ". . . we had to act with [great] dignity to keep them at all in their proper place," she said.[1]

In California, the native inhabitants were doubly scorned as "digger Indians," a term that came from their practice of digging edible roots and gathering nuts and berries for food. They lived in small bands that were more like extended families than tribes, with no laws, no currency, and no concept of ownership.

While interband fighting was not unknown, it could hardly be called warfare. The California tribes did not fight for food, because there was enough for everybody. There was no need to fight for land, either, because nobody owned it in the first place. They certainly did not fight for the strange yellow metal that white people valued so highly. Instead of admiring this peaceful lifestyle for its humanism and lack of greed, the whites labeled it savage.

Bayard Taylor's estimation of the native populations in California was fairly typical of the prevailing attitude:

> The small bands with whom I met, scattered through the lower portions of the foot-hills of the Sierra, and the valleys between them and the coast, seemed to be almost of the lowest grade of human beings. They live chiefly on acorns, roots, insects, and the kernel of the pine burr—occasionally they catch fish and game. They use the bow and arrow, but are said to be too lazy . . . to make successful hunters. . . . They have never pretended to hold any interest in the soil, nor have they been treated by the Spanish or American immigrants as possessing any. . . . It is possible that the government might, by collecting them together, teach them, in some degree, the arts and habits of civilization; but, if we may judge the future from the past, they will disappear from the face of the earth as the settlements of the whites extend over the country.[2]

Taylor was almost correct; the gold rush accelerated the destruction of California's native cultures, but it did not make them "disappear from the face of the earth." Some groups preserved their identity by moving away from the lands that interested the white newcomers. They drew upon their wildcrafting skills to survive in remote wilderness areas.

The African Americans

There is a gold-rush story that tells of a group of white miners in the town of Mokelumne Hill who decided to have a little fun with an African-American newcomer. He stopped one day and asked how to find promising digs. After pretending to consider the question thoroughly, the miners pointed out a barren hilltop, which had been prospected several times and never yielded so much as a dram of gold.

Try there, they said, best diggings in the territory. The man thanked them for their help and went off to dig himself a piece of the California dream. Within a few hours, the story had spread all over town, and everybody had a good laugh about the gullible man, up there digging on a played-out hill.

A week later, the African-American man came down from the mountain with a bag packed full of gold. When he stopped to thank the miners for their good advice, they did not have time to listen. They were off without a fare-thee-well, to do themselves some digging on that "played-out" hill.

When California became a state, the Thirteenth Amendment that would abolish slavery in the United States was still fifteen years away. Under the Compromise of 1850, California came into the Union as a free state, meaning that the buying and selling of human beings was forbidden by law. People could, however, bring in slaves they already owned, and any runaway slave captured in California could be returned to bondage. To further mollify the slaveholders, a delegate to the Constitutional Convention of 1849 wanted to prohibit free African Americans from entering the state:

> One of the first exciting questions was a clause which had been crammed through the Convention on its first reading, prohibiting the entrance of free people of color into the state. Its originator was an Oregon man, more accustomed to and better fitted for squatter life than the dignity of legislation. The members, by the time it was brought up for second reading, had thought more seriously upon the question, and the clause was rejected by a large majority; several attempts to introduce it in a modified form also signally failed.[3]

Admirable though this attitude might be, it did not mean that African Americans received full civil rights in gold rush California. They could not vote or testify in court, nor could their children attend school with

From the Compromise of 1850:

CLAY'S RESOLUTIONS
JANUARY 29, 1850

IT BEING DESIRABLE, FOR THE PEACE, CONCORD, AND HARMONY OF THE UNION OF THESE STATES, TO SETTLE AND ADJUST AMICABLY ALL EXISTING QUESTIONS OF CONTROVERSY BETWEEN THEM ARISING OUT OF THE INSTITUTION OF SLAVERY UPON A FAIR, EQUITABLE AND JUST BASIS: THEREFORE,

1. *RESOLVED*, THAT CALIFORNIA, WITH SUITABLE BOUNDARIES, OUGHT, UPON HER APPLICATION TO BE ADMITTED AS ONE OF THE STATES OF THIS UNION, WITHOUT THE IMPOSITION OF CONGRESS OF ANY RESTRICTION IN RESPECT TO THE EXCLUSION OR INTRODUCTION OF SLAVERY WITHIN THOSE BOUNDARIES. . . .

7. *RESOLVED*, THAT MORE EFFECTUAL PROVISION OUGHT TO BE MADE BY LAW, ACCORDING TO THE REQUIREMENT OF THE CONSTITUTION, FOR THE RESTITUTION AND DELIVERY OF PERSONS BOUND TO SERVICE OR LABOR IN ANY STATE, WHO MAY ESCAPE INTO ANY OTHER STATE OR TERRITORY IN THE UNION. AND,

8. *RESOLVED*, THAT CONGRESS HAS NO POWER TO PROMOTE OR OBSTRUCT THE TRADE IN SLAVES BETWEEN THE SLAVEHOLDING STATES; BUT THE ADMISSION OR EXCLUSION OF SLAVES BROUGHT FROM ONE INTO ANOTHER OF THEM, DEPENDS EXCLUSIVELY UPON THEIR OWN PARTICULAR LAWS.[4]

The Compromise of 1850 allowed California to enter the Union as a free state, but still allowed people to bring in the slaves they already owned.

white students. African Americans lived in a strange no-man's-land, threatened on the one hand by those who would return them to slavery and on the other by those who would give them freedom but not equality.

Some managed to make a life for themselves in spite of hatred and discrimination. Among those who succeeded in California were two outstanding men who had absolutely nothing in common beyond their African-American heritage.

James P. Beckwourth was strong and broadly built, with piercing, almost hypnotic eyes and undoubted courage. As pathfinder, guide, tracker, hunter, and occasional horse thief, the Virginia-born Beckwourth left a legacy of pioneer yarns that sound like something out of a story by Mark Twain or Bret Harte. Beckwourth blazed a trail across the Sierras, picking his way through wild, dangerous country to lay down a route that future pioneers could follow.

Mifflin W. Gibbs had a different sort of courage. He was an activist and self-educated journalist who cultivated the life of the mind. In 1855, he founded the first African-American newspaper in San Francisco, *The Mirror of the Times*, and built it into a successful and respected journal. In later life, he became the first African-American municipal judge in United States history and eventually served as American consul to Madagascar.

The African-American frontiersman James Beckwourth, discovered the trail that enabled gold rushers to cross the mighty Sierras.

The Latinos

The gold rush brought people from Mexico, Chile, and other Latin American countries into California for the same reason it brought them from the states: to look for gold. The memory of Mexico's crushing defeat in its war with the United States was still alive on both sides of the border. Mexicans in California met with the poisonous hatred reserved for conquered enemies, plus a general distrust of their culture. There was a heady, sensuous quality to Mexican life: intense colors, spicy foods, passionate music, and a language that could make a recipe for enchiladas sound like poetry. Americans found it threatening. In their minds, all Mexicans were either indolent peasants or brutal banditos like Joaquin Murieta.

Mexican-born Antonio Coronel neither fit the stereotype, nor was he a wealthy Californio, born to a life of privilege. He was a Los Angeles schoolteacher who decided to spend the summer of 1848 trying his luck in the town then known as Dry Diggings.

Luck was with Antonio Coronel that first summer. First, he met a priest who told him of good diggings on the Stanislaus River and had a bagful of gold to prove it. Coronel immediately headed for the Stanislaus, and was making camp on the main ravine when a group of Native Americans stopped to ask if he would sell his saddle blankets and serape, holding up bags of gold to show that they could pay. Coronel sold the serape and one blanket, then promptly moved his camp to where the Native Americans had been working. In three days, he dug more than eight pounds of gold. The next summer, Antonio Coronel was not so lucky. This time, he did go all the way to Dry Diggings, which by then was known as Hangtown. Perhaps the name change should have warned him. There was tension in Hangtown that year, and most of it was directed at the increasing number of foreigners coming to work the mines. California was a possession of the United States, the Americans said; its gold was therefore America's gold. Handbills were posted giving all noncitizens twenty-four hours to abandon their claims and get out of town.

Authority for this position came from Major General Persifor S. Smith. He was the commander in chief of United States Pacific forces. The previous January, in Panama, a steamship company had sold too many tickets for passage to San Francisco. General Smith's idea of solving the problem was to eject a group of Peruvian passengers and give their tickets to Americans. He dressed up his decision with legal-sounding gobbledygook and issued a written statement:

The laws of the United States inflict the penalty of fine and imprisonment on trespassers on the public lands. As nothing can be more unreasonable or unjust than the conduct pursued by persons not citizens of the United States, who are flocking from all parts to search for and carry off gold belonging to the United States in California; and as such conduct is in direct violation of the law, it will become my duty, immediately on my arrival there, to put these laws in force.[5]

Coronel was not about to be tossed out so easily. He joined with all the other noncitizens in Hangtown that year, and together they waited out the deadline. The Americans were not prepared to conquer this united front, but they could still make life uncomfortable for foreigners. Noncitizens were the first to be suspected of every crime, and the accusers were not inclined to be fussy about the rules of evidence or the rights of defendants.

Later that summer, a Frenchman and a Spaniard were charged with stealing four pounds of gold. The evidence against them was flimsy to say the least, but that did not stop a vigilante jury from sentencing them to hang. Antonio Coronel went to great lengths to help these men. He spoke out in their favor and even raised five pounds of gold from his fellow miners to repay the victim for his loss. None of it mattered. The vigilantes took the gold and hanged the men anyway. It was then that Coronel left the mining district for good, returning to his home in southern California and his life as a schoolteacher. A few years later, he became mayor of Los Angeles.

The Chinese

If the Mexicans were too flamboyant by Yankee standards, then the Chinese were too restrained and disciplined. Their culture was very old, steeped in tradition that westerners found puzzling and altogether strange. Physically, the Chinese made a stark contrast with the raw-boned Americans. They tended to be small and slightly built; their movements graceful and deceptively strong. Almond-shaped eyes lent their faces an air of mystery. Their alienness was so complete that Americans called them "inscrutable," which means mysterious and incomprehensible.

When there were only a few hundred Chinese in all of California, the term "inscrutable Oriental" was not meant as a slur, merely an observation. To Americans who had never seen an Asian before, nor observed what was considered their serene and strangely graceful culture, the Chinese *were* inscrutable. It was only later that the term became a cultural stereotype that implied secrecy and deception.

In 1850, civil strife in their homeland drove many more Chinese to try their luck in *Gum San*, the "Gold Mountains." They came by the thousands after that;

Chinese miners were patient and thorough. They made an abandoned claim profitable again.

20,026 arrived in 1852 alone. As their numbers increased, other miners began to see them as a threat.

They worked together in groups of about fifty men, sifting through diggings that had been abandoned by impatient Americans. Many a supposedly played-out claim became a profitable venture—a fact that rarely delighted the original owners, who had to live with the knowledge that they gave up too soon.

In addition to excelling in the mines, the Chinese remained aloof from American culture. Most of them planned to return to their homeland with their earnings, so they saw no reason to learn new and unfamiliar ways. All over gold country, little "Chinatowns" came into being.

Most have long since disappeared, but the famous San Francisco Chinatown still exists today as a functioning community. During the 1850s, it was not just an ethnic neighborhood, it was a separate world. In Chinatown, the laws and customs of America did not apply. It was a piece of Canton province, complete with gambling houses and opium dens, restaurants, temples, and rooms where diviners read fortunes in the pages of the ancient *I Ching* (*Book of Changes*). The pungent scent of soy sauce and peanut oil hung in the air, and up and down the streets one could hear the musical rhythms of Cantonese, with not a word of English to punctuate the flow.

As more Chinese companies spread through the mines, succeeding where Americans had failed, resentment flared into open hostility. Chinese were harassed, robbed, and even killed. The situation evolved into a vicious circle as harassment forced Chinese to band closer together for mutual defense, and this isolation in turn caused the resentment and misunderstanding that led to more harassment.

America's Gold

The general distrust of foreigners found expression in the Foreign Miner's Tax Law of 1850, which required all noncitizens to pay twenty dollars per month for a permit to conduct mining operations. The law caused such outrage that it nearly provoked a war between American and foreign miners before it was repealed in 1851.

Bigotry ran rampant everywhere in gold country. Throughout 1851–1852, lynchings and lashings became common, and the foreign born were the most frequent victims. In Downieville, a Mexican girl named Juanita or Josefa became the only woman ever lynched in the mines when she stabbed a white man who had insulted her. In San Francisco, the Committee of Vigilance lynched four men during 1851: three Australians and an Englishman.

Occasionally, cooler heads did prevail. In Sonora, a mob tried to hang four Mexicans who had been wrongfully charged with murder. The ropes were already on their necks when the judge, the sheriff, and several deputies came thundering through the mob and rode off with the prisoners. All four men survived to prove their innocence in a court of law.

At about the same time in that eventful summer of 1851, an old situation in San Francisco was winding down to a stranger-than-fiction conclusion. It started on July 2, when two men were searching for a thief who had just ransacked their house. They stopped a passing stranger, who made them suspicious the minute he opened his mouth: his accent was pure Sydney Duck, and his answers to their questions were strangely evasive. They took him to Vigilance Committee headquarters, where he gave his name as William Stephens.

Further questioning and investigation revealed his true name to be James Stuart. There was just one problem: James Stuart, alias Thomas Berdue, had been convicted of the infamous Jansen robbery and sent to Marysville, where a legally constituted jury found him guilty of murder. A hasty communiqué from the Vigilance Committee to the Marysville police quite literally saved Thomas Berdue's neck. He was cleared of all charges against him. His supposed partner, William Windred, was also cleared. Windred had already escaped from jail and made his way back to Australia, but the new verdict meant that he would no longer be a hunted fugitive. The real James Stuart became one of four men hanged by the Committee of Vigilance in the summer of 1851. In an interesting footnote to the case, when Charles Jansen and other witnesses saw both Berdue and Stuart, they agreed that there was not much resemblance between the two after all.

By 1852, the state legislature decided to have another try at the foreign miner's tax. This time, they set it at three dollars per month—enough to discriminate against noncitizens, but not enough to cause an uprising. With the tax, the lynchings, and the random violence, many foreigners did decide to leave the golden dream to the Americans who protected it so vigorously.

Latinos went back to Latin America, Australians to Australia, and the Spanish-speaking Californios lived in quiet isolation on their estates, hoping the insanity would somehow pass them by. Many Chinese also went back to their homeland. Those who stayed separated themselves more than ever from the violent Americans and their bottomless greed.

Oh my darlin'
Oh my darlin'
Oh my darlin'
  Clementine,
You are lost and gone
  forever,
Dreadful sorry,
  Clementine.

DREADFUL SORRY, CLEMENTINE

It was a simple fact of nineteenth-century life that women were defined by their relationship to men. There were wives and other "decent" women on the one hand, prostitutes and other indecent ones on the other. Any woman who did not fit into the first category was usually presumed to belong to the second.

In gold rush California, where people were making up the society as they went along, women had more freedom than they had in the states. They could not vote or serve on a jury, but they could own property in their own names. They had to be chaste, well mannered, and thoroughly domestic, but they did not have to be delicate porcelain dolls who could not do much of anything for themselves. Darlin' Clementine, after all, wore size nine shoes and drove ducklings to the water before she met her untimely end in that "foaming brine."

Wives, Mothers, and Marriageable Maidens

In the early years of the gold rush, women were so rare that the mere appearance of one in the street could cause a general uproar. A young Polish physician named Felix Paul Wierzbicki reflected on this situation in his book, *California as It Is, and as It May Be or A Guide to the Golden Region*:

> Women are very scarce; the domestic circle does not exist here as yet; domestic pleasures are wanting, and house-hold duties are unfulfilled. . . . We will, therefore . . . try to advocate the cause of poor and forlorn bachelors, and persuade some respectable heads of families that have daughters to settle in life, to come to California and build up the society, which, without woman, is like an edifice built on sand. Woman, to society, is like a cement to the building of stone; the society here has no such cement; its elements float to and fro on the excited, turbulent, hurried life of California . . . gold hunters. . . . Such is the society of San Francisco. But bring woman here, and at once the process of crystallization, if we may be permitted the expression, will set in[to] the society, by the natural affinities of the human heart. There are here many worthy men who . . . would like to be married and settled in life, as honest and sensible men should do; but for the want of the fair ones, they think only of getting away from here.[1]

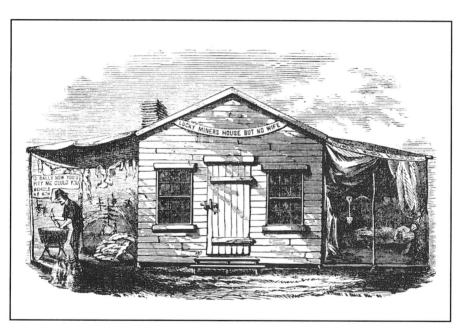

The lack of women during the early days of the gold rush became a prime topic of conversation—and complaint— among the miners.

SOURCE DOCUMENT

From a letter dated December 20, 1850:

THERE IS A WORLD OF LEGAL BUSINESS DOING AND TO BE DONE HERE, THIS IS ONE OF THE MOST SPLENDID CITIES FOR THE LEGAL PROFESSION IN THE WORLD. . . . YOU SEE NO WOMEN HERE. . . . IT IS A MOVING, JOSTLING, BUSY TIDE OF MAN IN HIS MOST EARNEST THROES FOR SUDDEN WEALTH. RIGHTS OF PROPERTY ARE RESPECTED, FOR THE INTEREST OF ALL EFFECTS THIS. BUT FOR TENDER SYMPATHIES . . . YOU MUST LOOK IN THE OTHER LANDS WHERE WOMAN HAS A MORE CONTROLLING AND HUMANIZING INFLUENCE.[2]

During the early years of the gold rush, the absence of women added to the disorderly atmosphere of the California mining towns.

The few marriageable women in gold country had their pick of suitors. Most waited in proper ladylike fashion for gentlemen to "come calling," then made their choice from among the available suitors. Miss Dorothy Scraggs used a more innovative approach, placing a notice in the newspaper:

A HUSBAND WANTED

BY A LADY WHO can wash, cook, scour, sew, milk, spin, weave, hoe, (can't plow), cut wood, make fires, feed the pigs, raise chickens, rock the cradle, (gold-rocker, I thank you, Sir!), saw a plank, drive nails, etc. These are a few of the solid branches; now for the ornamental. 'Long time ago' she went as far as syntax, read Murray's Geography and through two rules in Pike's Grammar. Could find 6 states on the Atlas. Could read, and you can see she can write. . . . Oh, I hear you ask, could she scold? No, she can't, you—good-for-nothing—!

Now for her terms. Her age is none of your business. She is neither handsome nor a fright, yet an old man need not apply, nor any who have not a little more education than she has, and a great deal more gold, for there must be $20,000 settled on her before she will bind herself to perform all the above . . .[3]

History does not record how Miss Scraggs fared in her search for a mate, but if candor and a rollicking sense of humor counted for anything, she must have done very well indeed. By modern standards her frank interest in money may seem harsh, but in 1850, a woman was entirely dependent upon her husband's income. She was expected to live within the means he could provide and make a home wherever he chose to live. For better or for worse, she shared his standing in the community.

Sarah Royce's husband never made his fortune in the gold fields nor was he a success in business. The family ended up living on the brink of poverty in the foothill town of Grass Valley. Sarah took solace in her home, her children, and her religion. She made the modest house into a refuge from the crudities of frontier living, and she took it upon herself to educate the children at home. Her youngest child, a son born in 1853, grew up to become the distinguished philosopher, Josiah Royce.

"Making do" was a necessity of life for many gold rush women, but not all of them managed as well as Sarah Royce. John Sutter's wife, Anna, had grown bitter and mean-spirited from her long years of living as a deserted wife. When their oldest son, August, wrote her about his father's success in America, Mrs. Sutter decided it was time to reunite the family. In January 1850, she presented herself and their three grown children to the husband she had not seen for sixteen years. The reunion was less than joyous; the Sutter children, twenty-two-year-old Eliza and her brothers Emil and Alfons, ages twenty and seventeen, scarcely remembered their father. Anna, however, remembered him all too well. He was paunchy now, and balding, but still the charming rascal she had married all those years ago.

Anna's timing, or perhaps her luck, was nearly as bad as her husband's. Instead of sharing his wealth and power, she arrived just in time to share his decline. In fact, she accelerated it by being rude and ill-mannered to his friends. While her husband was generous to a fault, Anna was stingy. She actually seemed to go out of her way to offend people. John Sutter withdrew into a private world of whiskey and memories.

The grim and humorless Anna Sutter eventually became her husband's sole companion.

Prostitutes and Dance Hall Girls

Prostitutes and dance hall girls soon followed the miners to the golden hills. These women were outcasts and "sinners," scorned by polite society. Because they had given up their right to be treated with the deference due a lady, men felt free to treat them in any way they pleased.

Some prostitutes drifted into their profession more or less on their own. Others were lured by the offer of legitimate work or even marriage. In Chile, a newspaper advertisement solicited two hundred girls—young, poor, and pretty—to go to California and be "honorably married" to wealthy miners. The advertisement did not say who had arranged this transport. There is no evidence that any of the girls actually got married. They probably ended up in bordellos (houses of prostitution).

Dance hall girls were generally not prostitutes, though their social standing was not a great deal better. In the early days of the fandango houses, Mexican and Mexican-American girls would be on hand to dance with the customers. However, the women could pick and choose their partners or leave if the party got boring. Sometime in the early 1850s, a clever promoter got the idea of bringing over country girls from Europe. He brought over women from Germany and France, to work as contract "hostesses" at dance halls all over gold country.

An article in the *Alta California* described the way the system worked:

> These girls receive shelter, food, raiment [clothing] and a gratuity of three hundred guilders, or about $240 per annum. They are hired out by the contractor to the various dance houses at the rate of $4 per night. . . . Their duties consist in waltzing or dancing with any man who may chance to drop in. The visitor approaches his partner, and without interchange of compliments, the girl . . . resigns herself to him . . . the music strikes up a lively air and off they rush in the giddy whirl. After a race of five minutes, the music ceases, and each girl marches her partner to the bar where he "treats." This duty performed, she is ready to repeat the same course with any one present. During her labors she holds no converse—it being a part of the business to avoid familiarity or even acquaintanceship.[4]

The arrangement doubtlessly helped to maintain order in the dance halls, but it relegated the women to the status of objects. It is probably no accident that the "contractors" chose girls who did not speak English. The lack of a common language served as a natural barrier to relationships.

Scandalous Ladies

The elite among these women of dubious virtue were the flamboyant misfits who were too classy to be common prostitutes and too scandalous to be respectable ladies. Eleanor Dumont shocked people all over gold country when she opened her own gambling hall in Nevada City. Her game was twenty-one, and she dealt it herself. Men gladly risked a week's earnings just for the novelty of gambling with the dark-eyed beauty who handled herself and the cards with unshakable poise.

Dancer Lola Montez practically started her own San Francisco fire when she made her stage debut in May 1853. Touring theatrical companies were just beginning to realize the potential of gold country. Miners would pay handsomely to forget their hardships for an evening and enjoy a play or musical variety show. It made them feel civilized again, reconnected to a life more refined and comfortable than the one they knew in the mines.

Montez gave them charm and beauty, with a delicious whisper of scandal to sweeten the experience. Born Eliza Gilbert in Limerick, Ireland, Montez was a natural beauty, with masses of black hair and wide, dark-blue eyes. As a dancer, she was untrained and undisciplined, and her acting was mediocre at best. Montez's real talent was not for playing theatrical heroines—it was for playing Lola Montez.

Montez invented herself many times over. In England, she married a second husband without bothering to divorce the first, and nearly went to prison for bigamy. In continental Europe, she captivated King Ludwig of Bavaria, provoked a revolution, and acquired the title Countess of Landsfeld. In California, she drew crowds with her famous "Spider Dance," a clever pantomime of a terrified woman trying to stomp out an invasion of spiders.

When her performing days were over, Lola settled for a time in the foothill town of Grass Valley. There she played hostess to a steady stream of writers, artists, musicians, and actors, who came together at "Lola's place" for the stimulating atmosphere and the chance to meet with others of like mind.

It was here in this small town that Lola Montez discovered the girl whose theatrical career would eclipse her own: Lotta Crabtree, "the airy, fairy, singing, dancing, miners' darling."[4] Lotta was only five years old when the Countess began teaching her the fundamentals of performing onstage. She was cute rather than beautiful, with a tumble of reddish curls and a bubbly charm that delighted even the most hardened audiences.

Lotta's first public performance was in a grimy mining camp that was known to live up to its name: Rough and Ready. Lola Montez lifted the little girl onto an anvil in a blacksmith's shop, so the miners could see her dance and sing. From that humble beginning, Lotta Crabtree became an international star, the first Californian ever to achieve that status.

Lotta Crabtree (left) and Lola Montez (right) packed theaters all over gold country.

Double Jeopardy

Nonwhite women faced prejudice based on race as well as gender. Those who dared to challenge the stereotypes paid a heavy price, as the strange life of Mary Ellen Pleasant shows. Born into slavery but freed at the age of nine, this daughter of a black mother and a white father became one of the most daring operatives in the Underground Railroad.

She helped dozens of slaves escape to freedom before an observant plantation owner discovered her true identity as an Underground Railroad operative. With the help of Marie LaVeau, notorious voodoo queen of the bayou, Mary Ellen escaped capture. She got out of New Orleans aboard a Panamanian steamer, bound eventually for the sunny shores of California. The year was 1848, and the timing was perfect; Mary Ellen arrived in San Francisco just as the gold rush began.

Here, the story of her life diverges. In one version, she was the mother of civil rights in San Francisco, fighting for the poor and downtrodden. In the other, she was "Mammy" Pleasant, a notorious bordello owner who practiced voodoo and exploited the people she pretended to help. Both versions agree that she amassed great wealth. By the time she had been in San Francisco for a few years, she owned a good chunk of city land along with farms, boardinghouses and livery stables.

Her boardinghouses catered to wealthy men who were either single or away from their families. She offered excellent food, elegant surroundings, and a place where gentlemen could entertain friends or business associates. Through her satisfied boarders, she built a network of contacts that put her at the very heart of San Francisco's power structure. Detractors claimed that she supplied her tenants with prostitutes on demand and "took care of things" if one of the girls got pregnant.

No one denies that Mary Ellen Pleasant possessed a shrewd intellect and a good amount of plain old common sense. The question is how did she put those qualities to use. In the early 1990s, historian Susheel Bibbs tracked down the background of this mysterious and often sinister figure from San Francisco's past.

Bibbs found that Pleasant was actually a civil rights activist who sheltered unwed mothers, runaway slaves, and ex-prostitutes who wanted a fresh start in life. She gave them food, lodging, and even vocational training, then used her boardinghouse contacts to place them in jobs. Detractors claimed that she had cornered the labor market, so she got paid by employers who needed workers, and by workers who needed jobs.

Mary Ellen Pleasant was reviled for "interfering" to help abandoned women negotiate support from their husbands who deserted them.

Being a realist who knew the way of things in a racially divided society, Pleasant largely ignored the gossips and rumormongers. They were part of the price she paid for being financially successful and supporting unpopular causes. The one thing she could not ignore was the demeaning title "Mammy." It smacked of slavery and the inferior status she'd worked a lifetime to escape. On her deathbed at age eighty-three, she was still railing against the injustice of it all.

Most gold rush women faced injustice of one sort or another, regardless of their race or station in life. Different women had different ways of coping: Mary Ellen Pleasant fought it, Lola Montez flaunted it, and Sarah Royce coexisted with it. Several thousand nameless prostitutes became its victims. With infinite variations of acceptance and rebellion, women survived the excesses of the gold rush and carved out a place for themselves in California society.

7

HOME AND OTHER UNFAMILIAR PLACES

The great California gold rush ended with neither a bang nor a whimper but in fits and starts, sputtering all the while. Fewer people came to California; more began to leave. Silent camps of weathered clapboard and tattered canvas dotted the hills like so many gravestones.

In an odd twist of fate, the forty-eighters lost a great deal more than they gained. The Californios lost their gracious way of life and their ancestral lands to Yankee greed. James Marshall, who started it all when he saw something shining in the water at Sutter's Mill, was never able to capitalize on his discovery. He died penniless and alone in 1885.

Even the irrepressible Sam Brannan came to a bitter end. By the mid-1850s, he was the richest man in California. One messy—and costly—divorce and several bad deals later, he was broke. When he died in

*This pioneer cemetery is a poignant reminder of the days
when gold was plentiful and dreams ran wild.*

James Marshall never profited from his discovery. Embittered and world-weary, he took to heavy drinking.

1889 there was not enough money in his estate to pay for his burial.

As for John Sutter, with his broken dreams and inconvenient family, California became a painful reminder of all he had lost. In 1870, he and Anna moved to Lititz, Pennsylvania, where she fulfilled one last wifely role, acting as nursemaid and sole companion to her alcoholic husband. Sutter died on June 18, 1880.

The gold rush was one of those rare events that passes into legend long before it passes into history. People who had been part of it told endless stories about the places they had seen and the things they had done. They had all been part of a time and a place where life outdid itself, and even the craziest dreams sometimes came true.

★ TIMELINE ★

1839—*January*: John Sutter arrives in California.

1846—*May 13*: Mexican War begins.

1847—*January 30*: Yerba Buena becomes San Francisco.

1847—*August*: James Marshall hired to build sawmill at Coloma.

1848—*January 24*: Marshall finds first traces of gold.

1848—*February 2*: Mexican War ends; California becomes part of the United States.

1848—*May 12*: Sam Brannan takes news of gold to San Francisco.

1848—*May 19*: First wave of miners (the "forty-eighters") flock to Sutter's Fort.

1849—*December 24*: First San Francisco fire erupts.

1850—*January*: Sacramento floods.

1850—*May 4*: Fire erupts again in San Francisco.

1850—*September*: Congress passed the Compromise of 1850; California becomes thirty-first state.

1850—*October*: A cholera epidemic begins in Sacramento.

1851—*February*: Jansen's drygoods store in San Francisco is robbed by E. M. Morgan and James Stuart.

1851—*March 15*: Berdue and Windred are found guilty of robbery of Jansen's store.

1851—*June 9*: The Committee of Vigilance is formed in San Francisco.

1851—*August 25*: Thomas Berdue is cleared of robbery and murder.

1851—*September*: The Committee of Vigilance is disbanded.

1852—Placer gold is exhausted. Many miners go home; women and families arrive in large numbers.

1853—The gold rush ends.

★ CHAPTER NOTES ★

Chapter 1

1. Richard Henry Dana, *Two Years Before the Mast,* In *Library of the Future,* 2nd ed. (CD-ROM) (Garden Grove, Calif.: World Library, 1991), 615–16:670.

2. John A. Sutter in Oscar Lewis, *Sutter's Fort: Gateway to the Gold Fields* (Englewood Cliffs, N.J.: Prentice-Hall, 1966), p. 147.

Chapter 2

1. William Ives Morgan, "The Log of a Forty-Niner," in *The West: A Collection from Harper's Magazine* (New York: W. H. Smith Publishers, 1990), p. 17.

2. Ibid., p. 16.

3. Ibid., p. 18.

4. Samuel Hazelton, "Violence From the Past: The Hazelton Letters," in *The Californians,* Mary Geneva Bloom, ed., vol. 12, no. 5 (Sonoma, Calif.: Grizzly Bear Publishing Company, n.d.), pp. 6–7.

5. Morgan, p. 18.

6. Bayard Taylor, *Eldorado, or Adventures in the Path of Empire* (Lincoln, Nebr.: University of Nebraska Press, 1988), p. 13.

7. John A. Stone, *Putt's Original California Songster* (San Francisco: Appleton & Company, 1858), p. 43.

8. Sarah Royce, *A Frontier Lady: Recollections of the Gold Rush and Early California* (Lincoln, Nebr.: University of Nebraska Press, 1977), pp. 3–4.

9. Stone, "Sweet Betsy from Pike," *Putt's Golden Songster*, p. 50.

10. In J.S. Holliday, *The World Rushed In* (New York: Simon and Schuster, 1981), p. 160.

11. Royce, p. 16.

12. Ibid., p. 72.

Chapter 3

1. Bayard Taylor, *Eldorado, or Adventures in the Path of Empire* (Lincoln, Nebr.: University of Nebraska Press, 1988), pp. 42–43.

2. William Ives Morgan, *The West: A Collection from Harper's Magazine* (New York: W.H. Smith Publishers, 1990), p. 18.

3. Joseph Henry Jackson, *Anybody's Gold* (New York: D. Appleton-Century Company, 1941), p. 83.

4. Poem is from a photo supplied Courtesy of the California History Room, California State Library, Sacramento, California.

5. Taylor, p. 119.

6. Ibid., pp. 238–239.

7. Ibid., p. 240.

8. J. Goldsborough Bruff in George W. Groh, *Gold Fever* (New York: William Morrow and Company, 1966), p. 144.

Chapter 4

1. "What Was Your Name in the States?" in Joseph Henry Jackson, *Anybody's Gold* (New York: D. Appleton-Century Company, 1941), p. 144.

2. Sarah Royce, *A Frontier Lady: Recollections of the Gold Rush and Early California* (Lincoln, Nebr.: University of Nebraska Press, 1977), p. 111.

3. George R. Stewart, *Committee of Vigilance: Revolution in San Francisco, 1851* (Boston: Houghton Mifflin, 1964), pp. 20–21.

4. "Pacific News," in Stewart, p. 41.

Chapter 5

1. Sarah Royce, *A Frontier Lady: Recollections of the Gold Rush and Early California* (Lincoln, Nebr.: University of Nebraska Press, 1977), pp. 10–11.

2. Bayard Taylor, *Eldorado, or Adventures in the Path of Empire* (Lincoln, Nebr.: University of Nebraska Press, 1988), pp. 340–341.

3. Ibid., p. 114.

4. From the Compromise of 1850, In Henry Steele Commager, *Documents of American History* (New York: Appleton-Century-Crofts, Inc., 1958), vol. 1, pp. 319–320.

5. General Persifor S. Smith in Donald Dale Jackson, *Gold Dust* (Lincoln, Nebr.: University of Nebraska Press, 1982), p. 81.

Chapter 6

1. Felix Paul Wierzbicki, *California as It Is, and as It May Be or A Guide to the Golden Region,* in *The Californians,* Mary Geneva Bloom, ed., vol. 12, no. 5 (Sonoma, Calif.: Grizzly Bear Publishing Company, n.d.), p. 28.

2. In J.S. Holliday, *The World Rushed In* (New York: Simon and Schuster, 1981), p. 308.

3. Dorothy Scraggs in Joseph Henry Jackson, *Anybody's Gold* (New York: D. Appleton-Century Company, 1941), p. 102.

4. *Alta California,* in Jackson, *Anybody's Gold,* p. 184.

★ FURTHER READING ★

Foley, Doris. *The Divine Eccentric: Lola Montez and the Newspapers.* Los Angeles: Westernlore Press, 1969.

Groh, George W. *Gold Fever.* New York: William Morrow & Co, 1966.

Jackson, Donald Dale. *Gold Dust.* Lincoln, NB: University of Nebraska Press, 1982.

Lewis, Oscar. *Sutter's Fort: Gateway to the Gold Fields.* Englewood Cliffs, NJ: Prentice-Hall, 1966.

Royce, Sarah. *A Frontier Lady: Recollections of the Gold Rush and Early California.* Lincoln, NB: University of Nebraska Press, 1977.

Taylor, Bayard. *Eldorado, or Adventures in the Path of Empire.* Lincoln, NB: University of Nebraska Press, 1988.

★ INDEX ★